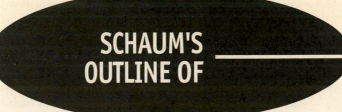

SCHAUM'S OUTLINE OF

Theory and Problems of

D0706247

XML

ED TITTEL
Austin Community College

Schaum's Outline Series

McGRAW-HILL

New York   Chicago   San Francisco   Lisbon   London   Madrid   Mexico City
Milan   New Delhi   San Juan   Seoul   Singapore   Sydney   Toronto

ED TITTEL has been an instructor at Austin Community College since 1996, where he teaches markup languages and networking topics. The author of over 100 computer books, and the originator of the Exam Cram certification preparation series. Ed also teaches various Windows topics at the NetWorld + Interop trade show. Feel free to e-mail Ed at etittel@jump.net.

Schaum's Outline of Theory and Problems of
XML

Copyright © 2002 by The McGraw-Hill Companies, Inc. All rights reserved. Printed in the United States of America. Except as permitted under the Copyright Act of 1976, no part of this publication may be reproduced or distributed in any form or by any means, or stored in a data base or retrieval system, without the prior written permission of the publisher.

1 2 3 4 5 6 7 8 9 10 11 12 13 14 15 16 17 18 19 20 VLP VLP 0 9 8 7 6 5 4 3 2

ISBN 0-07-138235-6

Sponsoring Editor: Barbara Gilson
Production Supervisor: Elizabeth J. Shannon
Editing Supervisor: Maureen B. Walker
Compositor: Keyword Publishing Services

Library of Congress Cataloging-in-Publication Data applied for.

McGraw-Hill
A Division of The McGraw-Hill Companies

PREFACE

XML is an abbreviation for the eXtensible Markup Language. It may be formally described as a second-generation metalanguage: second-generation because it represents a proper subset of a predecessor known as the Standard Generalized Markup Language (ISO Standard 8879, aka SGML); a metalanguage because like SGML, XML is a markup language designed to describe other markup languages.

In fact, XML excels at many things because it is so good at one thing: XML provides an open-ended, general-purpose tool that can be used to define ways of describing and capturing content of all kinds. That helps to explain why XML is used with equal facility to capture genetics data, family trees (genealogy), chemical and mathematical formulae, e-commerce transactions, and just about any other kind of technical or textual information that humans can think about.

This book is designed to supplement basic texts for introductory XML courses. This explains its early focus on XML syntax, structure, and semantics. It also explains its attention to various well-known document description techniques, including SGML Document Type Definitions (used to create most early and influential XML markup descriptions, including the first formal description of XML itself) and XML Schemas (itself an XML-based markup language designed specifically to describe other XML markup languages).

Likewise, the book's later chapters also cover important specific XML markup languages–often known as XML applications, in the sense that they represent specific language descriptions created using XML. These applications represent typical or important uses for XML-based markup languages that students are likely to encounter not just in course materials but also in the workplace. At best, these materials will help prepare you to work with specific XML applications; at worst, they will provide convincing demonstrations of XML's expressive power, broad capabilities, and fundamental simplicity.

The presentation of XML in this book assumes that students understand the basic principles that separate markup from related content. Early chapters establish a working vocabularly of markup elements, attributes, document descriptions, and so forth. Because this vocabulary is used throughout the XML community, and permeates the discussions and descriptions of XML applications in this book in particular, and in the standards and development communities that build and use XML-based markup languages, it's impossible to overstate how important it is to understand and master this vocabulary.

If basic introductory texts about XML are not included as part of the course for which this book is used, or you feel the need for a refresher on XML basics, the following references are highly recommended for further study:

1. *XML: Extensible Markup Language*, Elliotte Rusty Harold, Hungry Minds/John Wiley & Sons, Indianapolis, IN, 1998, ISBN: 0-7645-3199-9.

2. *Learning XML*, Erik T. Ray, O'Reilly & Associates, Sebastopol, CA, 2001, ISBN: 0-596-00046-4.

3. *XML Bible*, 2nd ed., Elliotte Rusty Harold, Hungry Minds/John Wiley & Sons, Indianapolis, IN, 2001, ISBN: 0-7645-4760-7.

ED TITTEL

CONTENTS

Introduction to XML

1.1   Origins and Description of the XML

The Extensible Markup Language (XML) was created in 1996 and is a subset of the Standard Generalized Markup Language (SGML). The design goals in the original World Wide Web Consortium (W3C) XML Working Draft document described a software-readable markup language intended for widespread distribution over the Internet that could be integrated into existing markup languages, such as the Hypertext Markup Language (HTML) and SGML, and still be easily readable by humans. This undertaking was quite a challenge, to say the least. Five years later, in February 1998, XML 1.0 reached W3C Recommendation Status and became one of the most talked about topics since the inception of the Web.

What makes XML so special? The key lies in XML's name itself: the Extensible Markup Language. The word *extensible* reflects that the language is flexible, scalable, and adaptable. XML can become anything that a document requires it to be for distributing information over the Web or between software applications—without the constraints and limitations of HTML.

By coupling XML documents with a Document Type Definition (DTD) or a schema document, the tags (or elements) used in the markup can be defined in unique and specific ways. They can be customized to a particular need and structured in a way that allows information to be exchanged in a language that is understood easily by software and humans alike. By creating rules and elements to meet the needs of the task, XML allows the exchange of structured data in an accessible yet easy-to-read format.

XML promises to meet the needs of a constantly expanding Web by meeting the limitations and shortcomings of HTML head-on. This chapter takes a look at a few HTML limitations to get a better sense of what XML has to offer. At the same time, a bit of markup language history is included.

The HTML standards have evolved rather slowly compared with the rate at which the Web changes. HTML has been behind the curve of the Web since the beginning and especially since the exponential growth and technical explosion of the past few years. The first widely used HTML standard was HTML 2.0, which was released in November 1995. The next incarnation was HTML 3.2, which became a recommendation in January 1997. Over 2 years later, in December 1999, HTML 4.01 became a recommendation. In January 2000, HTML was updated to incorporate features of XML with the release of the Extensible Hypertext Markup Language (XHTML). Each version of HTML built on the standards and practices of earlier versions, as well as incorporated browser-driven elements (elements created by browser vendors instead of the W3C). Updating the recommendations was in many ways the only viable approach to meeting the needs of the Web with the tools available, but it was definitely a game of catch-up. The HTML development cycle and recommendation process simply were too slow to keep up with the rapidly changing Web environment.

A side effect of the slow HTML evolution was the "browser wars" carried out by Netscape and Microsoft. The huge potential marketplace for Web-enabled software and the desire to incorporate the Web into the desktop and therefore achieve dominance in users' preferences and pocketbooks drove each company. The only way to capture the attention of the Web populace was to add proprietary elements to the HTML standards and hope that users would be so charmed by what the newest elements had to offer that they would forget about the competition.

The results of these skirmishes were manifold. First, the proliferation of browser extensions became a developer's nightmare. There were just too many combinations of possible elements, browsers, and user expectations. Something needed to be done before the situation spun out of control. A method was needed to define *just* the elements needed to do the job instead of trying to accommodate every conceivable possibility. XHTML arose from this "tag soup," meeting the needs somewhat but still not doing so as specifically as the new uses of the Web in business and information gathering required.

As more and more information was becoming available on the Web and was being exchanged via Web protocols, limitations were starting to appear in the capability of HTML to mark up data in a meaningful way. Although HTML was designed originally only to disseminate data, it quickly also became a way to present data; therefore, a content-meaningful markup was needed. HTML is adequate for presenting a document with style, images, hyperlinks, and the like, but it fails in the basic needs of data exchange.

An area of tremendous growth and research (and frustration for many) regarding HTML is in data searching and retrieval. As anyone who has used search engines knows, search phrasing is a dark science in and of itself. It seems that you find either too little or too much information depending on your skill, luck, or patience. What is needed is a way to identify meaning or context in a search—in other words, a means of organizing and identifying relevant information. In HTML, you use `meta` elements to mark keywords, dates, and so on, but this method is weak in comparison with XML. As more information of all types becomes Web-accessible, indexing becomes more critical, and only XML can meet this goal—as you will discover throughout this book. The ability of XML to point to a portion of a document and identify that bit of information in a meaningful way will be a tremendous boon to Web users (and search engines) everywhere.

Another spin-off of the browser wars has been the desire by the software giants to merge the Web and the desktop. With the browser becoming more of an application as well as a surfing tool, it grew in size, complexity, glitz, and glamour. What was needed was a simple, back-to-basics method of data exchange. It is not necessary to change the Web browser paradigm, but it is necessary to create a parallel structure that can blend into the Web as needed or remain separate and still be fully viable. XML meets these needs as a markup for content and data containers or through transformation, with the Extensible Stylesheet Language Transformations (XSLT), into fully presentable Web documents. An XML document can be tailored to suit the needs of the data and the application that requires those data.

XML avoids many, if not all, of the pitfalls that HTML has experienced by staying true to its basic design goals of data markup, extensibility, and the open-ended ability to adapt to a wide variety of applications and their future needs. As the Web expands further into new protocols, such as the Wireless Application Protocol (WAP), Wireless Markup Language (WML), Synchronized Multimedia Integration Language (SMIL), and the like, XML and its successors will adapt and evolve to meet those needs.

The implementation of XML has remained true to the original premise and promise of XML, which was to provide a content-driven language derived from and compatible with SGML, to provide the tools for Electronic Data Interchange (EDI) and other data-driven applications for which HTML was lacking, to be platform-independent, and to be distributed over the Web but not limited to the Web browser. This has been accomplished by strictly requiring key components of SGML that were optional in HTML and setting out and adhering to very stringent guidelines in XML.

1.2 Differences Between XML and HTML

Although HTML, XML, and (their hybrid) XHTML all use markup tags as containers for data elements and appear on the surface to be quite similar, the tags themselves are quite different not only in definition and meaning but also in their methods of creation and specification. Whereas HTML and its successor XHTML use elements that are more or less universally defined and accepted as HTML 4.01 or XHTML 1.0 (via the implied DTD that the browser includes), XML allows, encourages, and thrives on elements being created for structuring data to a specific intent and purpose. If an element is required for XML and is not part of the DTD being referenced, the author can create the element needed and define it for inclusion in the DTD specified in the XML document.

At the core, the differences between HTML and XML are very simple: HTML is a *presentation* markup language, readable and rendered by almost any modern Web browser, whereas XML is a *content* markup language, with no inherent, or built-in, presentation elements, only content-definition elements.

Note that the terms *tag* and *element* sometimes are used interchangeably, but they are not the same. An element is the opening and closing tag, its attributes, and its enclosed text or an empty tag and its attributes; for example, `<title>Outline of XML</title>` is an element. A tag is simply the opening or closing tag or the empty tag; for example, `<title>` is the opening tag and `</title>` is the closing tag.

The Web is an extremely powerful medium for the exchange of information, but unfortunately, HTML is not designed to accommodate a broad variety of data or datatypes. XML, because of its extensibility and derivation from SGML, is much more suited for data exchange (but without resorting to the complexity of SGML).

XML allows elements to be designed as an application-specific process, defined in a schema or DTD, and used over the Web in a language that best describes the data itself. By defining the XML elements needed, a number of otherwise nearly impossible tasks can be accomplished. Again, XML defines the data, and HTML defines the presentation. To put it another way, XML processes data, whereas HTML displays data.

Let's examine this simple yet crucial difference further to gain a greater sense of the respective power of the two languages. As anyone who has used HTML even casually knows, most of the elements have to do with the layout and look of the document—the presentation. Web professionals are all very familiar with such elements as `center` or `font` and so on. These elements (and other presentational elements) don't indicate the *type* of data contained. There are only a few HTML elements that do this. For Web pages, this is generally adequate, and use of these elements will continue to grow and thrive as the Web continues to expand. However, for indicating the type of data or their purpose, HTML falls a bit short with its minuscule number of content-related elements.

Because XML is intended as a content markup language, you can specify what the actual data is that is contained in the tags. For example, you might want to create a list of books that consists of the title, the author, the subject, the publisher, and more. There aren't any HTML elements that you can use to specify that the enclosed text is the name of the author.

XML doesn't have these limitations. You are relatively free to create the elements you need as long as you have them defined in a DTD or other document (such as a schema) that the reading software or agent can access. The story doesn't end here, however. Because XML is content-driven, you need to provide a method for presentation, which is addressed fully in later chapters. Suffice it to say here that you combine the XML document with a stylesheet—via the Extensible Stylesheet Language (XSL) or Cascading Style Sheets (CSS)—that defines how the content of each element is presented. The best part is that for software or agents that don't require presentation markup, you can simply provide the XML and the content it contains.

In practice, the differences for document authors are most important at the physical and logical levels, as well as the syntactical level. XML requires that you create well-formed documents. In addition, you can even check documents for validity. The tags used by XML elements are case-sensitive, whereas those used for HTML (at least in practice) are not. In addition, the treatment of attributes, as well as the need for quotations (you can use single or double quotation marks), becomes vastly more critical. To migrate from HTML to XML is not difficult, but the details are very important.

Here are some of the key differences between XML and HTML:

- XML is a *content* markup language; HTML is a *presentation* markup language.
- XML allows user-defined elements; HTML elements are predefined.
- XML requires validation; in HTML, almost anything goes.
- XML is data-driven; HTML is display-driven.
- XML allows data exchange between software applications; HTML is designed for visual presentation.
- XML is strictly defined and interpreted; HTML is very loosely interpreted.
- XML elements must be closed; in HTML, empty elements do not need to be closed.

1.3 Differences Between XML and SGML

SGML is one of the first languages to tackle the problem of transferring electronic data as marked-up text. SGML derives most of its power, and therefore its complexity, as a metalanguage, a language that describes and defines markup languages. The markup contained in SGML and its derivatives is described within SGML.

Traditionally, markup languages are made up of tags and elements used to describe data, either for presentation or as content. The system and meaning of tags or other annotations are described fully by the metalanguage that is applying them. Additionally, markup is expected to provide any system or methods of encoding of the data and describe how the encoding is to be interpreted.

SGML has been used extensively for technical documentation, government documents, and the like, but it is far too complicated for practical use on the Web. There are subsets and derivatives of SGML, however, that are perfectly adaptable for Web markup, such as XML, HTML, and XHTML. All these languages have a strong likeness to each other in syntax and markup conventions.

XML is closer to SGML in application, as well as in spirit, than HTML and is based very solidly on the concepts that have made SGML so powerful while still maintaining the look and feel of HTML. Because XML is extensible, it can define elements (using the proper DTD or schema) as needed for a specific document purpose or refer to a standard DTD.

XML shares four basic and important key points with SGML that are not available using HTML. These similarities are as follows:

- Each assembles a single document from many sources.
- Both define a document structure using a DTD or schema.
- Each adds markup to show the structural units in a document.

- Both can be validated to ensure that the document follows the structure defined in the DTD or schema.

Some of the key differences between SGML and XML are as follows:

- SGML is very complex; XML is simple.
- SGML documents always require a DTD; XML documents can stand alone.
- SGML software applications are expensive and complex; XML software is widely available, often as open source.

1.4   Uses of XML

Early uses of XML include documents for traditional Web browsers and industry-specific document exchange. Industries and disciplines such as chemistry, mathematics, real estate, weather observation, banking, electronic data interchange (EDI), and many more offer a vast potential use of XML. Because a DTD defines the XML document to be specific to the needs of the users, it may be adapted readily to any type of industry. For example, in the weather observation industry, the DTD can provide the elements needed for wind speed, pressure, temperature, humidity, and so on, which can be written by observer systems and then sent to and interpreted by forecasting systems. Because each element defines a particular type of content and the rules for its formatting, the documents are mutually understood and easily readable by a human. If the XML ultimately needs to be presented by a Web browser or other agent, the necessary XSL or CSS style sheet can be specified as well as rules for presentation, which pave the way for strictly defined elements and very narrow application within a specific industry or academic field. Many DTDs and schemas already exist for these applications, and others are being created constantly. XML will continue to evolve as more and more uses are discovered and implemented.

Wireless applications press XML into service in novel and very practical ways. The need to conserve bandwidth for—and format information on—a small, hand-held screen cries out for a simple, customizable data exchange media. XML can pass pure data or provide minimal presentation markup without all the excess baggage of HTML. Many flavors of XML will be developed that can meet the very narrow criteria of wireless display but expand into fully presented Web pages when the application requires it.

1.5   XML Document Structure

XML documents follow a very specific structure at several levels. One of the goals of XML stressed by the W3C was that "the design of XML shall be formal and concise." Every XML document has both a logical structure and a physical structure. A logical structure defines the use of elements, attributes, and other components employed in XML. The definition and declaration of the elements that make up the XML document are crucial to the success of the document and its viability with other documents. The physical structure encompasses the actual content of the document, consisting of the data and the elements that contain the data. In other words

- *Logical structure* defines the units and subunits of the data containers (the elements), defining datatype, attributes, and so on.
- *Physical structure* provides the data that goes into the elements, such as text, images, or other media, as allowed by the logical structure.

Well-formedness is part of the logical structure. For example, each document contains one, and only one *root*, or document element, that opens and closes the document. Within the root opening and closing tags, other elements are optional but are almost always present. These are considered to make up the logical structure of the XML document. Additionally, the logical structure contains declarations, entities, comments, character references, processing instructions, and the like. The first part of the XML document is the XML declaration, which specifies the XML version used, such as version 1.0, and whether it is a standalone document and the encoding. For example:

```
<?xml version="1.0" standalone="yes" encoding="UTF-8"?>
```

Looking at this markup a little closer reveals a few key points of information. First, `version` indicates that the document is using the rules set out by XML version 1.0.

What this indicates, on closer examination, is that the document is using XML 1.0, that there is not an external DTD (`standalone="yes"`), and that the document is using `UTF-8` encoding. This is the first logical entry. Following this XML declaration is the opening root tag, which is followed by the rest of the document and the closing root tag. Here is an example of a simple yet complete XML document:

```
<?xml version="1.0" standalone="yes" encoding="UTF-8"?>
<letter>
        <greeting>
        Hello there
        </greeting>
</letter>
```

To review and clarify the tag structure used in XML, an element opens with the familiar *<tag>* and ends with the *</tag>*. This is the same tag syntax used in HTML.

> Note that when you see text in italics within markup, that text is a placeholder.

This structure shows a basic physical and logical layout of the XML document. As the physical structure develops, you begin by adding the containers, or physical components of the document, following the logical structures that have been established.

The physical structure of an XML document is the structure of the actual data and information. XML documents share a logical structure, as defined by the schema or DTD, and then vary dramatically in physical structure based on the data they contain. In the preceding example, the logical `<greeting>`...`</greeting>` could contain "Hello there" or some other greeting as the physical structure.

Notice the nesting of the elements. The `<greeting>`...`</greeting>` tag pair is contained within `<letter>`...`</letter>`. This careful attention to the nesting of elements is part of what makes a well-formed XML document. With only the two elements contained in the preceding example, this document is simple and straightforward; however, as documents grow in complexity, the number of elements, nesting, and well-formedness becomes less apparent and easier to misplace.

In this section, let's add a couple more simple elements to the example, beginning with `signature`. Within `signature`, provide `message` and `name` elements. For the moment, do not be concerned with the types of entities in these elements, just their logical and physical placement in the sample XML document.

```
<?xml version="1.0" standalone="yes" encoding="UTF-8"?>
<letter>
    <greeting>
    Hello World!
    </greeting>
    <signature>
        <message>
        Most Sincerely. . .
        </message>
        <name>
        Joe Smith
        </name>
    </signature>
</letter>
```

Again, notice the nesting as shown by the indents. The `letter` contains both `greeting` and `signature`, and `signature` contains both `message` and `name`. Therefore, this is a well-formed document. If any of the element tags are out of sequence, for example, if the closing `message` tag and the opening `name` tags are transposed or overlap, the document is not well formed. As a further requirement for well-formedness, all attributes must be quoted, and attribute names should be unique. Finally, all elements should be closed, whether in pairs, as in this example, or as empty tags, such as `<subject name="example XML"/>`. Notice the slash and closing bracket (`/>`). This creates a single but complete tag. The familiar `<br>` tag in HTML would now be written as `<br/>` to be correct in XML. Note that for backwards compatibility reasons, you need to put a space before the closing slash in XHTML, for example, `<br />`.

Another important aspect of XML document structure is the use of entities. These represent reserved characters used to identify certain parts of markup. For example, the left angle bracket (<) identifies the beginning of a tag in markup. Therefore, if you want the parser (browser) to display a left angle bracket and not render it as markup, you need to use an entity. In this case, the correct entity is <. In XML, entities are also used to refer to often-repeated or varying text and might include the content of the external files through the use of pointers.

Entity references begin with an ampersand (&) and end with a semicolon (;). To use an entity, you can reference it by its unique name. Entity declarations allow you to associate a name with some other fragment of content that can be part of regular text, part of the DTD, or a reference to an external file containing either text or binary data. There are three kinds of entities in XML: internal entities, external entities, and parameter entities.

Internal entities are entities defined within the *same* document, whereas *external entities* are entities defined in a separate file. A *parameter entity* is one that can only be referenced within the markup declaration and usually is reserved for DTD designers. In addition, there are five predefined entity characters, which are listed in Table 1-1.

Table 1-1   The Five Predefined Entity Characters

HTML	Character	Description
&gt;	>	Greater than
&lt;	<	Less than
&amp;	&	Ampersand
&apos;	`	Apostrophe
&quot;	"	Double quote

These entities must be used in cases where markup is not intended, unless the text is defined as CDATA and contained in CDATA tags. They should be used whenever the characters are needed and they would conflict with the markup. Of course, other entities may be declared, but these are the only ones built into XML.

As a document grows in physical or logical complexity, the rules for well-formed XML still remain the same:

- Begin the XML document with a declaration.
- Provide at least one element (the root element) that contains all other elements.
- Nest tags correctly.
- Use both start and end tags for elements that aren't empty, and close empty tags properly.
- Quote all attributes.

Bear in mind that a document that is not well formed will not parse correctly and can cause an error on the parser; therefore, well-formed XML should be a basic goal. Keep in mind, however, that because a well-formed document does not have to adhere to any particular structure, the organization of the data is determined by how the data will be interpreted and used and compared with a DTD.

When an XML document is well formed and follows the rules of its specified DTD, it is said to be a *valid* XML document.

1.6   DTDs

The Document Type Definition (DTD) is the key to element meaning, attributes, logical structure, and context. It is required for a document to be valid. The DTD defines the elements that are used and the attributes they require and allows the document to be exchanged and understood by other software. A *DTD* is a set of rules that explicitly define the name, content, and context of each element. Therefore, the DTD is the foundation of an XML document, defining the template for how each image, link, and all other entities are processed. It is required for an XML document to be valid, as opposed to just well formed.

The DTD defines the building blocks (elements) that the XML document can use. A DTD can be declared in-line or as an external document. As such, the DTD allows the XML document to carry its own format description along with it or use a commonly available DTD via a Uniform Resource Identifier (URI). The basic building blocks of a DTD are as follows (each of these are defined, qualified, and described within the DTD):

- Elements
- Attributes
- Entities
- PCDATA
- CDATA

Much of this will be covered in greater detail in subsequent chapters. For now, let's take a look at these one at a time to get a better sense of what is used to create a DTD and therefore an XML document:

- *Elements*. The main blocks of HTML, such as `body` or `head`, and XML.
- *Attributes*. Information to further describe an element, such as `<body text="#000000">`.
- *Entities*. Variables to describe common text references.
- *PCDATA*. This means *parsed character data*. Think of PCDATA as the text contained between the start and end tags of an XML element. PCDATA is text that will be parsed by a parser. All text will be treated as markup, and entities will be expanded.
- *CDATA*. This means *character data*, but the text contained in a CDATA tag is not parsed, and markup is ignored.

Fortunately, you don't (usually) need to create a DTD from scratch. Many DTDs exist for XML authors and creators to refer to and access, and they are specific to the needs and practices of a particular purpose. Many DTD repositories and references can be found on the Web.

If you need to create a specialized DTD or simply want to explore the process, it is critical that you understand and properly define the entire scope and requirements of the document. You must note every nuance and either include or reject each. Because the language used is very simple, it is quite easy to master the actual DTD syntax; additionally, it is very useful to examine some common ones. DTDs consist of two key components: the element and the attribute. These two ingredients are essential to describing content and should be grasped fully.

In a DTD, XML elements are declared with an element declaration. The syntax is `<!ELEMENT element-name category>` or `<!ELEMENT element-name (element-content)>`. The usual structure of a DTD begins with a definition of the root element, and then definitions are narrowed down to the text level. Each required element is defined exactly and completely using a standard format. Here is a sample DTD for our example letter document:

```
<!ELEMENT letter (greeting, signature)>
<!ELEMENT greeting (#PCDATA)>
<!ELEMENT signature (message, name)>
<!ELEMENT message (#PCDATA)>
<!ELEMENT name (#PCDATA)>
```

Each element is named and takes the form `<!ELEMENT name content>`. If an element has attributes, they too need to be declared. Attributes often take the form `<!ATTLIST element-name name CDATA #IMPLIED>`. See Chapter 2 for a complete discussion.

1.7   Schemas

Schemas are employed with XML to identify a set of components for use in XML documents and to provide the rules for their correct combination. A schema is an XML-based alternative to a DTD that describes the structure of an XML document. Like DTDs, schemas define the following:

- Elements that appear in a document
- Attributes that appear in a document
- Elements that are child elements
- The sequence in which the child elements can appear
- The number of child elements
- Whether an element is empty or can include text
- Default values for attributes

This sounds just like a DTD, but schemas are intended as successors to DTDs. There are numerous preexisting schema languages, but the most well known is the W3C's XML Schema, released in May 2001. Some of the reasons that the W3C recommends XML Schema are as follows:

- It is easier to learn than DTDs.
- It is extensible to future additions.
- It is richer than DTDs.
- It supports datatypes.
- It supports namespaces.
- It is written in XML.

XML schemas improve on DTDs in several ways, including the use of XML syntax and support for datatypes and namespaces, both of which are invaluable for interfacing XML and databases. There are many instances in which a schema may be preferable to a DTD, but schemas are not intended to fully replace the DTD. In fact, there are many instances in which a DTD may be a better choice. For example, if the datatype is not critical, a DTD might be more economical to define and use, or perhaps a very workable DTD is already in place; therefore, the small advantage gained by the stricter schema might be negated by the current widespread use of a DTD.

If you are starting from the beginning, however, choices must be made as to the model selected. Schemas offer distinct advantages over DTDs in the area of data-typing, for example, a negative integer value as opposed to a simple integer value or the ability to define XML data to be the same datatype as a database field. Schemas allow a much more thorough description of the data contained in an XML document and require a much more thorough design. At times, a DTD would still be preferable, such as

- When you need a fairly compact definition
- When the data is primarily prose or readable text
- When nesting is more important than datatyping
- When the tools available simply do not support schemas

1.8 Validation

Whichever you choose, schemas or DTDs, the XML document must validate. Validation is something that might be new to most HTML authors because it is not required to create viewable and usable HTML documents. For the most part, if a document is displayed in a Web browser, it was valid enough. Keep in mind, however, that XML is intended to be read by software agents as well, and the tolerance for errors or ambiguity is much less. If there are flaws in the markup or it is incomplete, the document can and will fail to process correctly. Therefore, XML must validate in addition to the earlier-mentioned well-formedness.

Typically, an XML document is validated using an XML parser. The parser tries to read and interpret the document by following several steps. First, the document is tested for well-formedness. If any of the rules for a well-formed document are violated, the parser quits and returns an error. Passing this test, the document is then compared with a DTD, which is specified using a DOCTYPE declaration, for example:

```
<!DOCTYPE xml_example SYSTEM "xml_example.dtd">
```

The DTD must be accessible to the document in question, either locally or through a URI. All the XML document elements must be described by the referenced DTD or the document fails validation.

Validation for documents using a schema instead of a DTD is very similar. First, the document must be well formed. Then it is passed to an XML Schema parser, such as XML Schema Quality Checker by IBM, where the document is compared with the referenced schema and tested for validity. Failure again causes termination of the process and an error to be returned.

There are many parsers available for XML validation. For DTD-based XML, SAX and its derivatives are the de facto standard. SAX is based on Java and therefore quite portable to many platforms. XML parsers can be found in most popular programming languages, such as C, C++, Python, Perl, and others. Xerces, for example, is a C++ parser designed by the Apache group (`http://xml.apache.org/`). A common tool is the MSXML parser available from Microsoft and introduced in Internet Explorer 5.0. Additionally, there are parsers available online for uploading and validating XML.

1.9   Character Sets and Encoding

Because computers understand only numbers and what they represent, a document must be encoded for the character set that will reproduce it. Traditionally, the Web—and most of the documents that make up the Web—has been encoded in a character set known as Latin-1 or ISO-8859-1. This character set contains American Standard Code for Information Interchange (ASCII) code plus the accented letters and characters needed to represent most Latin-based alphabets, such as English, French, German, Spanish, and so on. Each character in the character set is referenced by 1 byte. Other common character sets include the Central European languages (ISO-8859-2); Esperanto, Turkish, and Maltese (ISO-8859-3); and the Cyrillic alphabet used for Russian and other Slavic languages (ISO-8859-5).

The default character set for XML is UTF-8, which is a Unicode character set. Basically, Unicode "specifies a unique number for every character, no matter what the platform, no matter what the program, no matter what the language"—this quote from www.unicode.org says it all. The aim is to provide a nearly universal character set to accommodate the wide variety of needs that XML can be designed to meet. Unicode is endorsed by such industry giants as Apple, Microsoft, Sun, Hewlett Packard, IBM, Oracle, SAP, Sybase, Unisys, and many others. It is incorporated into many operating systems and all modern browsers, as well as database tools (such as MS SQL Server, Oracle, and Sybase) and programming languages (such as Java, Perl, and Visual Basic).

Unicode is required by new technologies developed by such industry giants as the W3C, the Internet Engineering Task Force (IETF), and the Object Management Group (OMG). Examples are XML, XHTML, XSL, the Lightweight Directory Access Protocol (LDAP), and the like. UTF-8 is the most widely understood Unicode format and is the default encoding set for many programs that claim to use Unicode. In XML, however, the character set can be specified, the most common being UTF-8 or UTF-16. Table 1-2 provides some Unicode characters with their Windows and HTML encoding.

Table 1-2 Sample Unicode Characters with Windows and HTML Equivalents

Windows	HTML	Character Test	Description of Character
ALT-0130	‚	‚	Single low-9 quotation mark
ALT-0131	ƒ	ƒ	Latin small letter f with hook
ALT-0132	„	„	Double low-9 quotation mark
ALT-0133	…	…	Horizontal ellipsis
ALT-0134	†	†	Dagger
ALT-0135	‡	‡	Double dagger
ALT-0136	ˆ	ˆ	Modifier letter circumflex accent
ALT-0137	‰	‰	Per mille sign
ALT-0138	Š	Š	Latin capital letter S with caron
ALT-0139	‹	‹	Single left-pointing angle quotation mark
ALT-0140	Œ	Œ	Latin capital ligature OE
ALT-0145	‘	'	Left single quotation mark
ALT-0146	’	'	Right single quotation mark
ALT-0147	“	"	Left double quotation mark
ALT-0148	”	"	Right double quotation mark
ALT-0149	•	•	Bullet

ALT-0150	&#8211;	–	En dash
ALT-0151	&#8212;	—	Em dash
ALT-0152	&#732;	˜	Small tilde
ALT-0153	&#8482;	™	Trade mark sign
ALT-0154	&#353;	š	Latin small letter s with caron
ALT-0155	&#8250;	›	Single right-pointing angle quotation mark
ALT-0156	&#339;	œ	Latin small ligature OE
ALT-0159	&#376;	Ÿ	Latin capital letter Y with dieresis

1.10   Namespaces

Namespaces are a source of great confusion for XML students and many practitioners. The namespace concept is based on each element having a given set of attributes, with each attribute containing a name and value. There is no problem for element names that have no ambiguity or if there is no chance that an element may be used in a different context or meaning.

In HTML, the title tags mark up the section of text to appear in the browser title bar. There is no confusion here. However, what if you are combining two documents that both use the title element in different contexts, and neither of them relates to the HTML title element? Assume, for example, you are discussing books on genealogy, all of which have a (book) title, and the books are about family history, including royal families, which also have a title as part of the name element. How do you separate the book title from the royal title from the Web page title? You could rely on case sensitivity, but this is a poor fix. Instead, you use a namespace to define which title element is intended and how it is constructed.

Defining a namespace requires a bit more XML. The namespace syntax used in XML 1.0 is as follows:

```
<royalty:title
        xmlns:royalty="http://www.royalty.com/xml"/>
<genealogy:title
        xmlns:genealogy="http://www.genealogy.com/xml"/>
```

This allows you to declare where the namespace and declaration for each use of title reside, via the URI of each namespace referenced. To use the namespace, you can write the tag as <royalty:title> or <genealogy:title>, and the meanings are kept separate. In the preceding example, it would even be a good idea to add a declaration for `<html:title>` just to be consistent and complete. There are many techniques for scoping that may be applied, similar to other programming languages. *Scoping* refers to the property of a namespace that states that the namespace will be used throughout an element, including all elements that are within the element, unless overwritten by a new namespace declaration.

Namespaces should include the following four criteria:

- *Uniqueness*. The W3C's "Namespaces in XML Recommendation" provides XML users with ways to uniquely identify the vocabularies they are using inside documents.
- *Namespace identifiers*. Namespace identifiers use the URI syntax.
- *Prefixes*. A prefix can be created as shorthand for a URI.
- *Scoping*. Prefixes may be mapped based on URI for elements and their contents to avoid collisions.

For a full discussion, see one of the many online resources, such as the W3C's "Namespaces in XML Recommendation" at `www.w3.org/TR/1999/REC-xml-names-19990114/`.

1.11   Comments

The use of comments in XML probably will seem more familiar to you than some of the other topics covered so far. Comments in an XML document are more important than in most standard HTML documents—more along the lines of comments placed in mainstream programming languages such as Java or Visual Basic. The need for comments while learning XML is of great importance, and a succinct, readable commenting style is key to maintaining legible and understandable markup. It is very easy to forget the purpose of some simple task that you were sure you would never fail to remember, and the difficulty of recalling its purpose is directly proportional to the need to remember and inversely proportional to the amount of time you have to figure it out again. Therefore, be liberal with your comments, but keep them direct and to the point. Pretend that you are looking at your document for the first time. Would it make sense to you?

The syntax for comments in XML is very much like HTML and XHTML. XML uses the familiar `<!--` to start a comment and `-->` to end it. The same rules apply here as in the other markup languages:

- Comments may not appear inside any markup.
- Comments may not end with `--->` (three hyphens).
- Multiline comments are created automatically with one open and one closing tag.
- A double hyphen should not appear in any markup so as to maintain consistency with the comment syntax.

- Markup may appear inside a comment, that is, `<!--start the <root>` element `-->`.

1.12   Processing Instructions

Processing instructions (PIs) are allowed to contain instructions for an application that is processing an XML document. PIs have a target that identifies the target application, followed by the instructions. All PIs start with `<?` and close with `?>`. PIs can be used to indicate instructions that need to be passed to the application. Many PIs are used to specify a style sheet (XSLT) to be integrated with the XML document. Like comments, PIs are not textually part of the XML document and are not rendered as part of the document by the parser but rather are passed to the application indicated.

A PI is allowable anywhere in a document. The PI is equivalent to a server-side include instruction in HTML or a `meta` element directive, that is, instructions for a robot or other application that encounters the XML document.

To specify a style sheet, one would write a PI similar to the following:

```
<?xml-stylesheet href="mystylesheet.css"
      type="text/css"?>
```

This looks remarkably like the style directive used in HTML, with the `type` and `href` both declared. The `href` path, as in HTML, follows conventional URI rules. The following is an example of PIs for robots:

```
<?robots index="yes|no" follow="yes|no"?>
```

Any application that needs to be called by the XML file contains a PI. Multiple PIs are allowed, as per the W3C document, "Associating Style Sheets with XML Documents, Version 1.0" (`www.w3.org/1999/06/REC-xml-stylesheet-19990629/`). Some examples from that document are presented here with their HTML counterparts. These are style sheet directives. The XML PI is given first, followed by the HTML 4.0 equivalent.

```
<?xml-stylesheet href="mystyle.css" type="text/css"?>
<link href="mystyle.css" rel="style sheet"
      type="text/css">
<?xml-stylesheet href="mystyle.css" title="Compact"
      type="text/css"?>
<link href="mystyle.css" title="Compact" rel="stylesheet"
      type="text/css"/>
<?xml-stylesheet alternate="yes" href="mystyle.css"
      title="Medium" type="text/css"?>
<link href="mystyle.css" title="Medium" rel="alternate
      stylesheet" type="text/css"/>
```

Looking at these closely, it becomes apparent that XML is quite familiar to HTML authors, and very little rethinking is needed to put XML into practice.

1.13   CDATA Sections

CDATA is the most common attribute type, referring to character data, allowing the most freedom of character choice, and including URIs, monetary values, and symbols. CDATA can include any other text that is not in violation of the rules for a well-formed document. CDATA is used with normal text and normal character data.

CDATA is character data that might contain markup, but as text, not markup. This may not make sense at first, but if you need to refer to HTML from within XML, it is CDATA; therefore, the tags you are referring to are presented as text, not rendered. A CDATA section begins with `<![CDATA[` and concludes with `]]>`. The only markup recognized in a CDATA section is the concluding markup, the double square brackets and single angle bracket. Within the CDATA, you can use the `<` and `&` freely without resorting to the predefined entities `&lt;` and `&amp;`, respectively. This allows data containing these characters to be rendered as intended, as opposed to being interpreted. The parser ignores everything between the CDATA tags, including any comments or PIs.

Many elements are of the CDATA type, but you must bear in mind that text inside a CDATA section is ignored by the parser. Otherwise, all text in an XML document is normally parsed. If you place any markup inside a CDATA section, it is going to be ignored. This is far preferable to escaping every reference to markup, such as `<` and `&`.

1.14   xml:lang and xml:space

The two attributes of the XML namespace—`xml:lang` and `xml:space`—are reserved exclusively for XML. Both of these attributes are the keys to document presentation and readability. The `xml:space` attribute preserves white space in the physical layout, and `xml:lang` allows a mechanism for text to be translated and presented in a localized character set.

The `xml:lang` attribute creates a mechanism for an XML document to contain multilanguage text and, by using Unicode, to present documents with internationalized versions, including built-in translations. The `xml:lang` attribute allows the author to translate the Unicode XML to a specified character set. Each element potentially can have a different `xml:lang` attribute, although in practice this would not make much sense.

To use the `xml:lang` attribute, follow this example:

```
<quote xml:lang="en">
<!-- This is a quote in English -->
Time flies...
</quote>

<quote xml:lang="la">
<!-- This is a quote in Latin -->
```

```
Tempus fugit...
</quote>
```

The language code specified is a two-letter designation that is defined in ISO 639, "Codes for the Representation of Languages" (www.oasis-open.org/cover/iso639a.html). If you want to use an obscure language set and are not sure if it is specified, this is the document to check. Well over 400 languages are already specified, and if this is not enough, you can create your own (true to the XML spirit) as long as it is declared following standard practice.

White space has been a sore point for many versions of HTML because of its inherent tendency to reduce white space characters down to one space no matter how many were indicated. This affected spaces, blanks, tabs, and so on. The only option for HTML authors was the entity , but this required five characters to conserve one, not a very economical tradeoff. In XML, there is now an easy way to maintain this otherwise lost white space. This special attribute may be attached to an element to signal the intention that for that element white space should be preserved by applications. In valid documents, xml:space, like any other attribute, must be declared if it is used. When declared, it must be given as an enumerated type whose only possible values are default and preserve.

To maintain white space within a document, use the xml:space attribute in conjunction with XSL or CSS and as an attribute declaration:

```
<!ATTLIST element xml:space (default|preserve) 'choice'>
```

This is declared as part of an element declaration in standard fashion. The treatment of xml:space depends on the application being used—with browsers most likely to preserve the white space desired. Ideally, any document that specifies preserve should be presented verbatim, with all white spaces preserved, but this remains to be seen because it is very agent-dependent. The default behavior is to ignore white space (tabs, spaces, etc.). Therefore, the preserve behavior maintains the intended spacing and formatting that is desired.

1.15   XML Tools

XML and related tools fall into a wide variety of categories. The major groupings are

- *Editors*. There are editors for DTDs, schemas, and entire XML documents. These range from so-called what-you-see-is-what-you-get (WYSWIG) suites, familiar to users of HTML creation packages, to simple text editors with limited syntax highlight and interfacing to a parser/validator. Many of these are based on Java; therefore, they are platform-independent and will work with applications specific to Windows or other operating systems. Many of these tools are open source to encourage development by users and often are free to use.

- *Converters*. Converters are designed to translate documents from one markup language to another. These fall into several major categories also. One type allows conversion of non-XML documents into XML, such as a word processing document into an XML document. Another type will allow scripted conversion of documents from one XML type into another. A third group converts XML into a more widely used publishing format, such as Rich Text or LaTEX.

- *Parsers*. Parsers are available for most platforms, operating systems, and languages. The primary purpose of a parser is to parse and interpret XML documents. Not all parsers will validate documents, but each has a niche and specific purpose.

- *Storage and management*. Tools for document storage and management range from databases to search engines. This is an area of rapid development, with new tools becoming available quite frequently.

- *Delivery*. Document delivery is also an exciting area of development. This category includes publishing tools, Web browsers, and software agents. The browser wars of the earlier era of the Web may be ready for a rematch or another go-around for such standards as Scalable Vector Graphics (SVG), Synchronized Multimedia Integration Language (SMIL), and CSS. Meanwhile, there are a good number of tools to be tested and implemented while waiting for more broadly established standards. Some of these include Cocoon and PHP as document delivery systems and Amaya from the W3C, Internet Explorer, and Mozilla as Web browsers.

The following are available CSS editors, followed by the platform on which they run:

css-mode Emacs	
HTML-Kit	Win32
Dtddoc	Python
DTDParse	Perl
LiveDTD	Perl
perlSGML	Perl

The following are available DTD editors, followed by the platform on which they run:

ezDTD	Win32
tdtd	Emacs

The following are available DTD generators, followed by the platform on which they run:

Data Descriptors by Example	Java
FirstSTEP	Win32
Rhythmyx XspLit	Win32
SAXON	Java
XMI Toolkit	Java 1.2

The following are available DTD parsers, followed by the platform on which they run:

CL-XML Common	Lisp
DTD Parser	Java
DTDParser	Perl
DTDParser	Java
PXP	Objective Caml 3.00
xmlproc	Python 1.5

The following are available integrated development environments (IDEs), followed by the platform on which they run:

XML and Web Services DE	Win32

The following are available schema converters, followed by the platform on which they run:

DTD2RELAX	Java

The following are available XSL checkers, followed by the platform on which they run:

XSL Lint	Perl
XSL Trace	Java

The following are available XSL converters, followed by the platform on which they run:

XSL to XSLT Converter	Win32

The following are available XSL editors, followed by the platform on which they run:

HTML-Kit	Win32
XPath Tester	Java 1.2
XSL Editor	Java
XSL Tester	Win32
xslide	Emacs

The following are available XSLT generators, followed by the platform on which they run:

Rhythmyx XspLit	Win32
WH2FO	Java

Document Type Definitions

2.1 Document Type Declarations

Every Extensible Markup Language (XML) document needs a blueprint, a foundation that defines what each element in the document means and what is appropriate, proper, and understood within the context of the XML document. By definition, XML encourages the custom use and definition of tags; therefore, some method to map elements to meaning is required.

The current most common type of tool for element declaration is the *Document Type Definition* (DTD). The DTD has been in use since the Standard Generalized Markup Language (SGML, developed in 1988). Although the Hypertext Markup Language (HTML) and its derivatives use DTDs (rather transparently because they are built into the browser), XML has brought common use of the DTD back to the forefront of Web development. You need to gain a solid working knowledge of the DTD to be able to fully exploit the subtleties and power of XML.

In the XML processing instruction (also called the *prolog*), you define the document to be one of two types: standalone (`standalone="yes"`) or not standalone (`standalone="no"`). Standalone documents (`standalone="yes"`) do *not* require a DTD, although one can be used as long as it is consistent with and doesn't change the content of the XML document. The default value of the `standalone` attribute is `no`, which requires that a DTD be present.

A DTD can be declared as either *internal* or *external*. An external DTD is stored as an American Standard Code for Information Interchange (ASCII) text file with the file extension `.dtd` and is meant to be shared with other XML documents via the Web. An external DTD is specified by a Uniform Resource Identifier (URI) in the prologue. An internal DTD is inserted within the document type (DOCTYPE) declaration. DTDs used in this way are limited to the specific document.

The DTD provides the rules that a *parser* (the software tool interpreting the document) must follow for validation and proper interpretation. Structurally, the DTD also follows strict rules to ensure that the desired results are achieved and the data is rendered properly.

The DTD is the key to element meaning, attributes, logical structure, and context of the XML document. It is *required* for a document to be *valid*. The DTD defines the elements that are used and the attributes they require and allows the document to be exchanged and understood by other software. A DTD is a set of rules that explicitly define the name, content, and context of each element. Therefore, the DTD is the foundation of an XML document, defining the template for how each image, link, and all other entities are processed. It is required for an XML document to be valid as opposed to just well formed.

The DTD defines the building blocks (elements) that the XML document can use. A DTD can be declared in-line or as an external document, or the XML can be treated as standalone. A parser will look for the indicated DTD for validation and return an error if it is not found or does not make sense. One of the great benefits of the DTD system is that it allows the XML document to carry its own format description along with it or use a commonly available DTD via a URI. Often XML documents that are interchanged within a specific industry or academic discipline will share a common DTD, developed specifically for said purpose, that is accessible to all. An important side effect of a common DTD is that as the DTD evolves, it is constantly being reflected as an updated resource that all the documents can share, further extending one of XML's strongest assets: its extensibility. Centralized repositories for DTDs are becoming more commonplace, whether as a URI on the Web or limited to a local-area network (LAN). Before designing an XML document or a DTD, be sure to do some research to determine if the DTD already exists and if it is suitable or adaptable for your XML needs.

We shall review the basic building blocks of a DTD as follows. Each of these is defined, qualified, and described in the upcoming pages:

- *Elements*. The main components of HTML and XML.
- *Tags*. Characters used to enclose the elements.
- *Attributes*. Information to further describe an element.
- *Notations*. References to helper applications or plug-ins.
- *Entities*. Variables to describe common text references.
- *PCDATA*. Parsed character data, which is the text within an XML element's start and end tags.
- *CDATA*. Character data, indicated by the CDATA tag. This data is not parsed.

We'll examine each of these one at a time and take a close look at where each part fits into the DTD and, in turn, the XML document.

We'll create a motion picture DTD. As you plan your DTD, it is helpful to create a simple outline. This helps you see the relationships and types of data you wish to declare, as well as helps you prevent omissions. As you create the outline, don't worry too much about the structure of the data; you can reorganize your data before creating the DTD. Just make a list.

For our motion picture DTD, we list key points first (and some quick notes, if desired) and then add structure and detail in turn. Here are the key points:

- Title
- Year
- Genre
- Director
- Distributor
- Cast
- Music
- Run time
- Country
- Language
- Medium
- Certification

Each of these points *might* represent an element. Elements are essential to DTDs and XML because they provide the logical structure of the document. The element provides the skeletal foundation and components of the XML document. Each element contains the *name* of the element, any *attributes* it possesses, and the *datatype* it contains. An element has a *start tag,* nearly identical to those found in HTML, and an *end tag,* again like most HTML tags. However, a new twist comes about with the empty element tag. Whereas in HTML you could write empty tags without closing them, for example, `<br>`, in XML you write empty tags with a closing slash at the end, for example, `<br/>`. This serves the function of opening *and* closing within the same tag. You also can use opening and closing tags with empty elements (`<br></br>`), but this is not done very often. Consistent with the requirements of well-formed XML, all tags must be complete, with an opening and a closing. The empty tag just described meets this requirement.

Consistent still with HTML, attributes contained in the element are closed by implication; that is, a `<body>` tag that has, say, three attributes needs to be closed only once, as in `</body>`.

The basic element declaration is structured like this:

```
<!ELEMENT element_name (datatype)>
```

An element can contain attributes, which are name-value pairs within a tagged element that modify certain features of the element. An attribute specifies the type (and value) of additional parameters that can be contained in the element. For XML, all values must be enclosed in quotation marks. Either single or double quotation marks are acceptable; just be consistent. Attributes are defined in the DTD as a subset of the element definition. The syntax for the attribute is very similar to the element:

```
<!ATTLIST element_name attribute_name type default_value>
```

In our motion picture example, an element will be declared for the film. This would be written as:

```
<!ELEMENT motionpicture (title, year, genre, director, cast, music)>
```

This declares that the `motionpicture` element is made up of the following elements: `title`, `year`, `genre`, `director`, `cast`, and `music`. We'll have more on elements and attributes later in this chapter.

The DTD is parsed and compared with the XML document as part of the validation process. All elements and other components are inspected, and relationships between them are established. Validation is crucial, so you need to be confident that the document is correct, that all the elements are included and identified, and that the overall logical structure is sound. If there are any errors or omissions, the parser will indicate this and usually return an error or just not display the document correctly. The comparison/validation process is especially critical when documents are shared between software applications, more so than when simply rendered to a Web browser.

Bear in mind that validation still requires the XML documents to be well formed. If the document fails the well-formed test, validation also will fail. Remember that *well formed* means that the tag structure follows the rules for syntax and completeness outlined in the DTD. Validation is therefore a two-step process: Check the document for well-formedness, and compare it with the DTD.

Before we go too much further in our discussions, we should look at symbols used in DTD construction, as well as some syntax rules and conventions, as shown in Tables 2-1 through 2-3.

Table 2-1   Some Common Symbols Used in
DTD Construction

Symbol	Definition
?	One or none
*	Wildcard: one, many, or none
+	At least one required, many allowed
,	Separates list items
|	Alternation (either or)
&	Entity
%	Parameter entity

Table 2-2 Elements with Their Syntax and Rules

Element	Example	Description
#PCDATA	`<motionpicture (#PCDATA)>`	The `motionpicture` element contains parsed character data, or text.
#PCDATA, *element-name*	`<motionpicture (#PCDATA, title)>`	Contains parsed character data and another element named `title`. #PCDATA *always* appears first in a rule. In this case, the comma inside the rule indicates that `motionpicture` *must* contain text *and* the `title` element.
, (comma)	`<motionpicture (title, year, genre)>`	When commas separate two or more arguments, it indicates *their order*. Here, `motionpicture` must contain the `title`, `year`, and `genre` elements in that order.
| (bar or pipe)	`<motionpicture (title | year | genre)>`	The pipe symbol specifies *either/or*. Here, `motionpicture` has one of the following elements: `title`, `year`, or `genre`.
title (by itself)	`<motionpicture (title)>`	When an element occurs by itself it may be used one time *only*. Here `motionpicture` must contain a `title`, used exactly once. Note: this implies that no occurrence indicator symbol means "use one time only."

? (question mark)	`<motionpicture (title, year?, genre?)>`	The question mark symbol means use the marked element(s) either zero or one times. Here `motionpicture` must contain `title` exactly once, followed by zero or one `year`, and zero or one `genre` elements.
+ (plus sign)	`<motionpicture (title+, year?, genre)>`	The plus symbol means use the marked element(s) one or more times. Here, `motionpicture` must contain at one or more `title` elements, zero or one `year` elements, and one `genre` element.
* (asterisk)	`<motionpicture (title*, year?, genre)>`	The asterisk means use the marked element(s) zero or more times. Here, `motionpicture` contains zero or more `title` elements, followed by zero or one `year` elements, and one `genre` element.
( ) (parentheses)	`<motionpicture (#PCDATA | title)*>`	Parentheses define groupings, and may be multiple levels deep. Here `motionpicture` contains zero or more uses of *either* or *both* parsed character data and `title` elements.

	`<motionpicture ((title*, year?, genre)*	genre)>`	Here, `motionpicture` may contain zero or more instances of the items in the first internal group of parentheses or a single `genre` element. If the initial group is chosen, it can include zero or more `title` elements, zero or one `year` elements, and a single `genre` element. This entire group may also be repeated zero or more times.
	`<motionpicture (title | year)+>`	Here, `motionpicture` must include at least one `title` or `year`. The plus sign outside the parentheses means that `title` or `year` may appear once or may repeat as many times as needed.

Table 2-3 Attribute Rules

Attribute	Syntax	Description
CDATA	`<ATTLIST genre category CDATA #REQUIRED>`	Character data, text that is not parsed. The `genre` element has an attribute named `category`. This attribute contains letters, numbers, or punctuation symbols and is required.
NMTOKEN	`<ATTLIST genre category NMTOKEN #REQUIRED>`	Name token, text with some restrictions. The value contains numbers and letters. It cannot begin with the letters `xml`, and the only symbols it can contain are `_`, `-`, `.`, and `:`. The `genre` element has a required attribute named `category`. This attribute contains a name token.

(value-1 | value-2 | value-3) value list	`<ATTLIST genre category (drama | scifi | comedy | other) "other">`	A value list provides a set of acceptable options for the attribute to contain. In general, you always should include "other" as one of the options. The genre element has an attribute named category. The category can be drama, scifi, comedy, or other (default).
ID	`<ATTLIST genre category ID #IMPLIED>`	The keyword ID means that this attribute has an ID value that identifies this particular element. The genre element has an attribute named category. The category will contain an ID value. ID and IDREF work together to create cross-referencing of elements.
IDREF	`<ATTLIST genre category IDREF #IMPLIED>`	The keyword IDREF means that this attribute has an ID reference value that points to another instance's ID value. The genre element has an attribute named category that contains an IDREF value. ID and IDREF work together to allow cross-referencing of elements.
ENTITY	`<ATTLIST genre category ENTITY #IMPLIED>`	The keyword ENTITY means that this attribute's value is an entity. An entity is a value that has been defined elsewhere in the DTD to have a particular meaning. The genre element has an attribute named category that will contain an entity name rather than text.

NOTATION	```<ATTLIST genre category NOTATION #IMPLIED>```	The keyword NOTATION means that this attribute's value is a notation. A notation is a description of how information should be processed. You could set up a notation that allows only numbers to be used for the value, for example. The genre element has an attribute named category that will contain a notation name.

2.2   Notations

The notation type attribute is somewhat rare. One use for notation would be to define a *helper application* or *plug-in* to accommodate the datatype specified in the notation declaration. For example, if an image datatype requires a special image viewer, then we can state the location of the application, as well as any other parameters. An example of this is

```
<!ELEMENT map EMPTY>
<!ATTLIST map image ENTITY #REQUIRED>
<!ENTITY map1.png SYSTEM
        "http://www.anysite.net/map1.png" NDATA png>
<!NOTATION png SYSTEM "file:///C:/Program
        Files/mapviewer.exe">
```

or more commonly

```
<!NOTATION GIF89A SYSTEM "GIF">
```

When the browser or other software encounters the element `<map image= "map1.png"/>`, these facts are known:

- The browser knows that image is a valid attribute.
- If the attribute value is map1.png, the file is found at www.anysite.net/ map1.png.
- They are binary data of type png.
- Binary data of type png is handled by the program mapviewer.exe on the C drive in the Program Files directory.

The helper application `mapviewer.exe` is called, and then the image file can be viewed. Most Web browsers can handle the `png` file type, but if a nonstandard image format is needed, we have a method for handling it.

The `NOTATION` in the previous markup could be applied to any type of binary data, such as word-processed files, spreadsheets, or databases. As long as the helper application is declared in a valid fashion, as in the example, and the application called for is in the correct path, any datatype can be included in the XML document.

2.3   Entities

Entities in general allow an XML document to draw on many resources, some of which are transient or dynamic. By drawing on different files, one of the true powers of XML is tapped. These pieces of information are called *entities*. It might be easier in some cases to think of an entity as a macro for programmers, as a pointer to more complex functions, or even as a function call itself. No matter which model you use, the entity allows a dynamic insertion of text or other data into the document at hand.

We used another attribute in the previous example, the `ENTITY` attribute. An entity can be thought of as a type of shorthand or name of an unparsed entity declared elsewhere in the document. In Chapter 1 we saw an example of predefined entities for the <, >, and & characters. These are built in as part of the XML language, but as is always the case, we can declare our own entities. The `map1.png` entity we referred to in the preceding example allows us to reference the full path of the image file simply by using the `entity` value. As in HTML, the name of the entity is preceded with an ampersand (&) and followed by a semicolon (;).There are three types of entities: *internal, external,* and *parameter*. An internal entity has the replacement text or data (that it represents) stored elsewhere in the same declaration and document. For example, if we declare the following:

```
<!ENTITY MH "McGraw-Hill">
```

we can use `&MH;` to insert `McGraw-Hill` in its place as shorthand. Internal entities allow you to define shortcuts for frequently typed text or text that is expected to change, such as the revision status of a document. If we declare an entity for `Revision Number` using the following markup, you can simply reference `&RN;` and update every instance of the revision number without having to search and replace throughout the entire text:

```
<!ENTITY RN "Revision Number">
```

An entity is always referenced with the ampersand and the entity name. If you want to use a literal ampersand (&), you have to use the predefined entity `&amp;`. If you don't, the parser will look for a reference to an entity. If you wanted to refer to Samson & Delilah, you would have to type `Samson &amp; Delilah`, or you could create the following entity and use `&SD;` instead:

```
<!ENTITY SD "Samson & Delilah">
```

The XML specification predefines five commonly used internal entities. Refer to Table 1-1 in Chapter 1 for a review of these entities.

XML documents use external entities, which can contain binary or text data, to refer to external files. If an external entity contains text, that text is inserted in the XML document at the point of reference and parsed as part of the referring document. Binary data is *not* parsed and may be referenced only in an attribute. Binary data is used to reference images, media clips, and other non-XML (or text-based) content in the document. For binary data, a notation might be needed to describe the appropriate helper application or plug-in. To locate an external entity, you use a standard URI reference, a path, or a fully qualified name.

Parameter entities appear only within DOCTYPE declarations, where such an entity may be recognized by the percent sign and the space (%) that precedes its name in a declaration. Likewise, this percent sign appears in references to parameter entities later on in the DOCTYPE body. When a processor interprets this text, parameter entities are immediately replaced with their substitution text as defined in their initial declarations, whereas normal entity references are not expanded. This allows you to create far more readable element and attribute declarations, especially when ampersands and other markup are included. Using parameter entities allows an element declaration to be built of smaller, more manageable units and allows changes to be made across the entire DTD more easily.

2.4   IGNORE and INCLUDE

IGNORE and INCLUDE allow the DTD developer to test or debug sections of a DTD structure. These keywords function like a switch, turning elements on or off as needed. They also allow more control over the flow of the DTD when it is being debugged. However, these keywords are rarely found in production. If you need to combine several DTDs into a single unit, these controls are indispensable for tracking down collisions and conflicts. These two keywords seem to be falling out of favor in production XML, as vestiges of SGML, and are used infrequently outside the SGML realm.

2.5   XML Content Models

The actual content that makes up an element or attribute follows a *content model,* which uses a form of symbol shorthand to describe the structure of the data within the tag itself. The easiest way to grasp this is to view some examples of common element types and then break them down into what they are describing.

The symbols used most commonly in content models are shown in Table 2-4. The occurrence indicators used in content models are shown in Table 2-5.

Table 2-4 Symbols Used in
Content Models

Symbol	Description
,	Indicates a sequence
|	Indicates an alternation
( )	Indicates a grouping

Table 2-5 Occurrence Indicators

Symbol	Description
[nothing]	Element occurs once
?	Element is optional and can occur once if used
+	Element can occur one or more times
*	Element can occur zero or more times

If #PCDATA appears in a content model, it has to appear first and only once. In addition, if it is an alternation, you can only use the * (zero or more times) occurrence indicator. In addition, you have these other options:

- #REQUIRED. Must be present; return an error if empty.
- #IMPLIED. Optional; may be ignored if no value.
- #FIXED *value*. Every instance of that element must have that value.
- EMPTY. Does not contain data, only markup.

We'll look at a list of element tags, all with slightly different characters, and then determine the meaning of each:

- `<!ELEMENT a (b+)>` describes an element named a with a child element b that appears one or more times.
- `<!ELEMENT b EMPTY>` describes an element named b as an EMPTY element.
- `<!ELEMENT c (#PCDATA)>` describes an element named c, as PCDATA, that appears once.
- `<!ELEMENT a (b,c)>` describes an element named a with b and c elements that each appear once and in this order.
- `<!ELEMENT a (b|c)*>` describes an element named a with a b *or* c element that appears as many times as needed.
- `<!ELEMENT a (#PCDATA|b|c)*>` describes an element named a, with PCDATA, a b element, or a c element that can appear as many times as needed.

- `<!ELEMENT a (b, (c|d)*)>` describes an element named a with a b element that appears once and then a c *or* d element that can appear as many times as needed.
- `<!ELEMENT a (b?, (c|d)+)>` describes an element named a with an optional b element and then a c *or* d element that can appear one or more times.
- `<!ELEMENT a (b?, (c+|d+))>` describes an element named a with an optional b element and then a c *or* d element that can appear one or more times each.

2.6 Element Structure

Before moving forward, look back at the motion picture key points. We made the following key point elements:

```
title
year
genre
director
cast
music
```

The following key points would make better attributes because they are descriptive and nonessential:

```
certification
runtime
country
language
medium
```

To determine whether to create an element or an attribute, decide whether you need to search for a particular part of the document (element) or if you are just providing detail to an existing bit of data (attribute). For example, the `title` data would seem a most likely candidate for an element, whereas `medium` might be better as an attribute of `title` or some other element. Table 2-6 shows the main points that should be declared as elements and notes potential attributes for each.

Table 2-6   Elements and Attributes for the Motion Picture Example

Element	Possible Attributes
`<! ELEMENT title (#PCDATA)>`	language, alternate title, country, certification, runtime
`<! ELEMENT year (#PCDATA)>`	academy_awards, distributor
`<! ELEMENT genre (#PCDATA)>`	category, medium
`<! ELEMENT director (#PCDATA)>`	director_of_photography, cinematographer, Editor

Here is the XML document so far, showing some of the declared elements:

```
<motionpicture>
    <title>"The Wizard of Oz"</title>
    <year>1939</year>
    <genre></genre>
</motionpicture>
```

This example shows just the logical structure provided by the elements declared thus far in the `motionpicture` element. This will work as XML if you indicate the appropriate DTD, but it is hardly comprehensive. For instance, there is no `medium` (in this case, both black and white and color) included, nor is there much said about the music, including the classic "Somewhere Over the Rainbow." Should you add more elements and create attributes to describe the details? There are proponents for both methods, both lumpers and splitters. The *lumpers* clump together elements with a lot of attributes, whereas the *splitters* tend to create separate elements for every data element. A good deal of thought should go into the outline of a DTD so that the XML document can be as efficient as possible yet still be complete. For the motion picture example, we'll try to navigate the middle ground.

As our criteria, we'll set the data that is fairly fixed in time and space as elements, with one primary value for each element, and use attributes to provide details and optional information. As an example, we'll create the `title` element (which is usually a given) but allow an alternate title (or more if need be) as an attribute value. Along with the attribute for an alternate title, we'll include the language that the film is produced in, the country of origin, the certification(s) it has been awarded, and so on. None of these is critical to the actual title, but they are of interest and importance as details. We could easily create an element for country of origin, and this would be very important for a DTD of international motion pictures, but for our example, as well as for most filmgoers, this is a side note. The same goes for language and certification, although, again, depending on the use of the XML document, these could be given element status. For a DTD of educational motion pictures, these both would be of more importance.

The `year` element is fairly straightforward, with the `academy_awards` and `distributor` attributes provided for historical perspective, again as attributes and thus optional. The same goes for genre, with perhaps medium as an attribute or an alternate genre value. As we add music, director, and most of all, cast to the elements, the structure of the DTD and the XML documents begins to take shape.

Let's look at the element list so far:

```
title
year
genre
director
distributor
cast
music
```

We've dropped several earlier list items from elements and changed them to attributes. This evolution of the DTD is not unusual because it will clarify the structure of the DTD. If we are creating a DTD for our own XML documents, we can continue to adjust the structure as we see fit as long as the XML is still valid. However, the time spent in planning the DTD will pay off in the long run as more and more documents are designed using the DTD without requiring any modification. It is like the old carpenter's adage, "Measure twice and cut once."

2.7 Attribute Structure

We should begin our examination of attributes by looking at a few of the rules for their use and a few conventions as well. The attribute structure allows us to qualify an element and further refine or define the data it conveys.

First, attributes are not mandatory. They may be declared as such or they can be optional. This is stated in the element declaration itself by referencing an attribute to an element by name; for example:

```
<!ELEMENT title (#PCDATA)>
<!-- Declare an attribute alternate_title for title
        element -->
<!ATTLIST title alternate_title CDATA #IMPLIED>
```

What this says to the parser is that for the title element, we can have an alternate_title attribute that consists of CDATA (character data) and is optional (indicated by the notation #IMPLIED). If we would like to include a default value, such as none, we would replace #IMPLIED with the string none.

Second, we can use multiple ATTLIST statements to declare multiple attributes for the same element. For more than one attribute, we would list them all, referencing the element name and declaring a unique attribute name. Recall that in the original outline we noted language, alternate_title, country, certification, and runtime as potential attributes for the title element. Expanding on the previous markup, the attribute list for motionpicture becomes

```
<!ELEMENT title (#PCDATA)>
<!ATTLIST title language CDATA #IMPLIED>
<!ATTLIST title alternate_title CDATA #IMPLIED>
<!ATTLIST title country CDATA #IMPLIED>
<!ATTLIST title certification CDATA #IMPLIED>
<!ATTLIST title runtime #IMPLIED>
```

Attributes might be set as required or optional or have a fixed value. In our example, we use #IMPLIED, which makes the attribute optional. To require the attribute, we replace #IMPLIED with #REQUIRED, and if the attribute is not present, the parser will return an error.

So far all the attributes for title have the same datatype, which is CDATA. However, we can indicate another datatype during declaration, such as PCDATA, ID, or ENTITY. For our example, CDATA is sufficient, although we might be able to use a reference or two as shorthand. Later in this section we will discuss the various appropriate datatypes.

This structure is repeated for each element in turn, setting the various data-types and adjusting the default values to suit the data contained. For the motionpicture element and its child elements, we see a structure like so:

```
<!ELEMENT motionpicture (title, year, genre, director)>

<!ELEMENT title (#PCDATA)>
    <!ATTLIST title language CDATA #IMPLIED>
    <!ATTLIST title alternate_title CDATA #IMPLIED>
    <!ATTLIST title country CDATA #IMPLIED>
    <!ATTLIST title certification #IMPLIED>
    <!ATTLIST title runtime #IMPLIED>

<!ELEMENT year (#PCDATA)>
    <!ATTLIST year academy_awards CDATA #IMPLIED>
    <!ATTLIST year distributor CDATA #IMPLIED>

<!ELEMENT genre (#PCDATA)>
    <!ATTLIST genre category CDATA #IMPLIED>
    <!ATTLIST genre medium CDATA #IMPLIED>

<!ELEMENT director (#PCDATA)>
    <!ATTLIST director director_of_photography CDATA
        #IMPLIED>
    <!ATTLIST director cinematographer CDATA #IMPLIED>
    <!ATTLIST director editor CDATA #IMPLIED>
```

Some of the qualities attributes possess are

- The name of the element
- The namespace of the element/attribute

- The type of data or the attribute type, such as ID, IDREF, IDREFS, ENTITY, ENTITIES, NMTOKEN, NMTOKENS, NOTATION, CDATA, and ENUMERATED
- The default value, if any
- Whether an attribute is #REQUIRED or #IMPLIED and how many instances are permitted or required

Here are a few other simple key points to keep in mind when deciding whether to use elements or attributes:

- Too many attributes can make a document hard to read.
- The document structure cannot be described by using only attributes; elements are required.
- Attributes are best for simple information; for more complex information, an element is better.

2.8 Building Document Structures

XML (and the DTD) follows two distinct models for the document structure. We have the physical structure of the document and the logical structure. In some ways, the *physical* and *logical* labels might be confusing, so perhaps we can think of them as *layout* and *syntax*.

Looking at the physical structure (layout) first, we are presented with the *storage units* or *containers* of the data. The physical storage of an XML document can be visualized as a set of files or other components. Look at these as the building blocks of the document—what the overall document is made up of.

In the case of the motionpicture XML document, we have the following structure:

```
<motionpicture>
    <title></title>
    <year></year>
    <genre></genre>
    <director></director>
</motionpicture>
```

This is shown diagrammatically including attributes in Figure 2-1. This diagram, or map, allows you to see the physical structure of the data without having to define it logically (syntax). More important, it allows you to view the data as units, or chunks of information, so that you can determine that they are comprehensive and contain all the data our XML requires. You are not concerned yet with declarations, elements, comments, character references, and processing instructions, all of which are indicated in the logical structure, just the actual containers themselves.

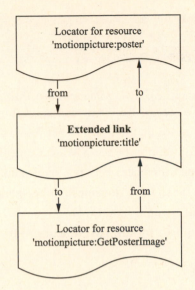

Fig. 2-1. Diagram of the `motionpicture` XML example.

At this point, if we are missing a key data container, we should add it to the physical map of the document or its DTD. Once we are satisfied with the makeup and completeness of our data requirements, we can start to define them syntactically as the document's logical structure.

The individual units that are defined as parts of the physical structure are now broken into their components, such as elements, declarations, and so on as the document's logical structure. Each element is described, and in turn, any and all attributes or other details and requirements that comprise the physical unit are declared, including default values, datatypes, and the like. This process defines what the element *is*, how it is constructed, what it consists of, and the rules that it must follow. The logical structure describes how the data is defined and manipulated and serves as the real workings, or mechanics, of the document without regard to how the element fits into the overall document.

The rules for the logical structure are the same rules as those used for elements, attributes, entities, and the like, and the requirements for a well-formed document also must be followed (tag structure and syntax). The document might require validation, depending on the original processing instructions, which has an impact on the logical structure as well. If flaws are found in the document, either as to its well-formedness or through validation, they will be reported by the parser and will need to be repaired. This does not reflect on the physical structure of the document, only the logical structure. Syntax errors, datatype collisions, and failure of validation are all aspects of the logical structure.

Review Questions

2.1 If the prologue (the opening line and processing instructions) of the XML document states `standalone="no"`, how is the location of the DTD indicated?

2.2 Can there be more than one DTD per XML document?

2.3 What is the foundation of the XML document?

2.4 What are some differences between an element and an attribute?

2.5 Is a DTD required for a document to be validated?

2.6 What is meant by an in-line DTD?

2.7 A DTD is required for an XML document to be
   a. Valid
   b. Well formed
   c. Parsed
   d. All of the above

2.8 How is a DTD shared between XML documents?

2.9 Name two types of industries or academic disciplines where a common DTD is available.

2.10 Can a DTD be edited?

2.11 Binary data is not parsed. True or false?

2.12 What type of tag is used for a helper application?

2.13 What type of entity appends a DTD?
   a. Internal
   b. External
   c. Parameter
   d. All of the above

2.14 How is a parameter entity identified?

2.15 Are `IGNORE` and `INCLUDE` commonly used in XML?

2.16 What is the purpose and use of each of the following symbols in a DTD?
   a. *
   b. ,
   c. ?
   d. |

2.17 Is an attribute mandatory?

2.18 How do you indicate an optional attribute?

Problems

Create a DTD and an XML document for a simple music collection.

2.1 Use the artist's name, the name of the work, the genre of the work, and any other details.

2.2 Define elements and attributes.

2.3 Create a DTD (in-line).

2.4 Create the prologue for the document.

2.5 Create a well-formed XML document.

Answers to Review Questions

2.1 In standard URI syntax, either as a local path or fully qualified URI.

2.2 Yes, there can be multiples as long as namespace conventions are observed.

2.3 The element.

2.4 Elements provide the basic building blocks of the document; attributes further describe elements.

2.5 Yes, it is required for validation.

2.6 The elements are declared within the XML document.

2.7 **a.** A DTD is required for an XML document to be valid.

2.8 By referencing the address in the processing instructions.

2.9 Examples: academics, aerospace, automotive, computers and electronics, financial services, health care, insurance, petrochemicals, retail, telecommunications, and utilities/energy.

2.10 Yes, just like any other document.

2.11 True.

2.12 NOTATION.

2.13 **d.** All of the above.

2.14 A parameter entity is identified by placing a percent sign and a space (%) in front of its name in the declaration.

2.15 No, they are more specific and common to SGML.

2.16 * is a wildcard meaning one, many, or none; , separates list items; ? means one or none; and | means alternation (or).

2.17 Only if #REQUIRED.

2.18 #IMPLIED.

Solutions to Problems

2.1 Determine the logical structure of the XML document. Decide on the root element, any other elements, and attributes. In this case, use CD as the root.

2.2 The elements will be title, song, artist, and composer. The attributes will be genre, year, and length.

2.3 Here is a suggested DTD and the element order:

```
<!ELEMENT CD (title, artist+, song*)>
<!ELEMENT title (#PCDATA)>
<!ELEMENT artist ((firstname*, lastname) | group?)>
<!ELEMENT firstname (#PCDATA)>
<!ELEMENT lastname (#PCDATA)>
<!ELEMENT group (#PCDATA)>
<!ELEMENT song (#PCDATA)>
<!ATTLIST song genre CDATA #IMPLIED>
<!ATTLIST song year CDATA #IMPLIED>
<!ATTLIST song length CDATA #IMPLIED>
```

2.4 `<?xml version="1.0" standalone="yes" encoding="UTF-8"?>`.

2.5 An XML document using the in-line DTD:

```
<?xml version="1.0" standalone="yes" encoding="UTF-8"?>
<!DOCTYPE title [
<!ELEMENT cd (title, artist+, song*)>
<!ELEMENT title (#PCDATA)>
<!ELEMENT artist ((firstname*, lastname) | group?)>
<!ELEMENT firstname (#PCDATA)>
<!ELEMENT lastname (#PCDATA)>
<!ELEMENT group (#PCDATA)>
<!ELEMENT song (#PCDATA)>
<!ATTLIST song genre CDATA #IMPLIED>
<!ATTLIST song year CDATA #IMPLIED>
<!ATTLIST song length CDATA #IMPLIED>
]>
<cd>
<title>Beautiful Maladies</title>
<artist>
<firstname>Tom</firstname>
<lastname>Waits</lastname>
</artist>
<song genre="urban folk" year="1987" length="2:42">
    Hang on St. Christopher</song>
<song genre="urban folk" year="1987" length="3:51">
    Temptation</song>
<song genre="urban folk" year="1985" length="3:45">
    Clap Hands</song>
</cd>
```

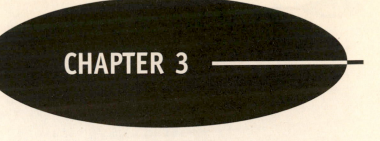

CHAPTER 3

Schemas

3.1 Basic Schema Concepts

Document Type Definitions (DTDs), the common validation tool for Extensible Markup Language (XML) document models, have been around since the Standard Generalized Markup Language (SGML). Although DTDs have several advantages, long-standing implementation being one of them, there are also several disadvantages. The following are some of the disadvantages often associated with DTDs:

- They follow a different syntax than XML.
- They lack detailed datatyping.
- Declarations are difficult to read and understand.

The alternative designed to address DTD shortcomings was proposed by the World Wide Web Consortium (W3C) and is formally called the XML Schema Language. Although XML Schema is a more complex language, it allows the document author to define strict datatypes for both element and attribute values.

The basic concepts that underlie XML Schema are similar to those for XML DTDs. The main function is the same: validation. For example, consider an online educational company's enrollment progress report. The data is collected class by class. An XML Schema defines strict hierarchy and datatypes for the data and therefore enforces document structure and data integrity. The following is an example of an XML document using enrollment data:

```
<?xml version="1.0"?>
<enrollment
      xmlns="http://www.lanw.com/namespaces/enrollment">
   <class>
      <title>XHTML Part I</title>
      <period name="Session 1">125</period>
      <period name="Session 2">67</period>
      <period name="Session 3">115</period>
```

```
    </class>
    <class>
        <title>XHTML Part II</title>
        <period name="Session 1">110</period>
        <period name="Session 2">89</period>
        <period name="Session 3">122</period>
    </class>
    <class>
        <title>XHTML Part III</title>
        <period name="Session 1">87</period>
        <period name="Session 2">44</period>
        <period name="Session 3">77</period>
    </class>
    <class>
        <title>An Introduction to XML</title>
        <period name="Session 1">101</period>
        <period name="Session 2">88</period>
        <period name="Session 3">112</period>
    </class>
    <class>
        <title>Transforming XML with XSLT</title>
        <period name="Session 1">90</period>
        <period name="Session 2">69</period>
        <period name="Session 3">102</period>
    </class>
    <class>
        <title>XML Content Management and Delivery</title>
        <period name="Session 1">67</period>
        <period name="Session 2">55</period>
        <period name="Session 3">82</period>
    </class>
</enrollment>
```

The following would be a corresponding XML Schema document:

```
<schema xmlns="http://www.w3.org/2001/XMLSchema"
        xmlns:enr="http://www.lanw.com/namespaces/
        enrollment"
        targetNamespace="
        http://www.lanw.com/namespaces/enrollment">
<element name="enrollment">
    <complexType>
        <element ref="enr:class" minOccurs="1"
        maxOccurs="unbounded"/>
    </complexType>
</element>
<element name="class">
    <complexType>
```

```
    <sequence>
        <element ref="enr:title"/>
        <element ref="enr:period" minOccurs="1"
        maxOccurs="unbounded"/>
    </sequence>
</complexType>
</element>
<element name="title" type="string"/>
<element name="period" type="string"/>
    <complexType>
        <attribute name="name" type="string" use="default"
        value="unknown"/>
    </complexType>
</element>
</schema>
```

3.1.1 SPECIFICATION DOCUMENTS

XML Schema is defined formally by two documents maintained by the W3C: the Structures Recommendation and the Datatypes Recommendation. In addition to these two recommendations, there is a third primer document that illustrates schema concepts (www.w3.org/TR/xmlschema-0/). To fully understand XML Schema, you must be familiar with the two primary XML Schema recommendation documents:

- *XML Schema Part 1: Structures*. The first part of the standard defines methods for describing the structure and constraining the contents of XML documents; it also defines the rules governing schema validation of documents. The most recent version was defined on May 2, 2001. You can find this document at www.w3.org/TR/xmlschema-1/.

- *XML Schema Part 2: Datatypes*. The second part defines a set of simple datatypes that can be associated with XML element types and attributes. This allows XML software to do a better job of managing dates, numbers, and other special forms of information. The most recent version also was defined on May 2, 2001. You can find this document at www.w3.org/TR/xmlschema-2/.

3.1.2 SYNTAX

One of the advantages to using XML Schema is that it follows XML syntax rules and therefore can be parsed by an XML parser. These syntax rules are

- All nonempty elements must have an opening and closing tag.
- All empty elements must be terminated: <empty/>.
- All attributes must have values, and those values must be in quotation marks.

- All elements must be nested correctly.
- Elements and attributes are case-sensitive.

3.1.3 NAMESPACES

Whereas DTDs are not namespace-aware, XML Schema takes advantage of namespaces and uses them often. There are two schema-dedicated namespaces:

- `http://www.w3.org/2001/XMLSchema`. Namespace used for W3C XML Schema elements. This namespace can be used as a default namespace or with an `xsd` prefix. If you use the `xsd` prefix, every schema element needs to adorn the prefix as well (for example, `<xsd:element>...</xsd:element>`).

- `http://www.w3.org/2001/XMLSchema-instance`. Namespace used for W3C XML Schema extensions employed in instance documents. This namespace should be defined with an `xsi` prefix. You do not need to use this namespace unless you will be using XML Schema extensions.

In addition to the two schema-dedicated namespaces, you can declare your own namespaces to correspond with the declared elements and attributes. Using what is known as a *target namespace*, you can define a namespace to which the corresponding XML document should adhere. For example, if you want an XML document to adhere to a particular namespace (see the following example), such as `http://www.lanw.com/namespace/enrollment`, you can define that requirement using a target namespace in the corresponding schema document. For example, you could create the following XML document:

```
<?xml version="1.0"?>
<enrollment
      xmlns="http://www.lanw.com/namespace/enrollment">
   <class>
      <title>XHTML Part I</title>
      <period name="Session 1">125</period>
      <period name="Session 2">67</period>
      <period name="Session 3">115</period>
   </class>
   <class>
      <title>XHTML Part II</title>
      <period name="Session 1">110</period>
      <period name="Session 2">89</period>
      <period name="Session 3">122</period>
   </class>
</enrollment>
```

A DTD does not support namespaces, and although you can define an `xmlns` attribute with a fixed value (for example, `<!ATTLIST enrollment xmlns CDATA FIXED "http://www.lanw.com/namespace/enrollment">`), it does not truly represent a namespace. However, XML Schema allows you to define the namespace, for example:

```
<schema
      targetNamespace="http://www.lanw.com/namespace/
      enrollment">
.
.
.
</schema>
```

Working with namespaces can be a tricky matter; just remember that you must use the XML Schema namespace, and you can create a target namespace for the resulting XML document.

3.2   Advanced Schema Concepts

Before we cover element and attribute declarations, you need to be familiar with both complex and simple type declarations.

3.2.1   COMPLEX TYPE

An element is defined as a complex type if it allows for child elements and/or may take attributes. There are two ways to define complex types. First, you can create a complex-type definition that can then be used in an element type declaration. Each complex-type definition can contain element declarations, element references, and attribute declarations. For example, the following is a complex-type definition:

```
<complexType name="fullnameType">
    <sequence>
        <element name="firstName" type="string"/>
        <element name="lastName" type="string"/>
    </sequence>
</complexType>
```

This example creates a complex-type definition that can be used in various element declarations. For example, now you can create an element named customer that must follow the fullnameType definition. (In other words, it must always have firstName and lastName child elements.) For example:

```
<element name="customer" type="fullnameType"/>
```

The second way to declare complex types is to define them as a part of the declaration itself. In this case, you do not define a complex type that you reference later. You use a complex-type definition directly within the element declaration itself; for example:

```
<element name="customer">
```

```
<complexType>
    <sequence>
        <element name="firstName" type="string"/>
        <element name="lastName" type="string"/>
    </sequence>
</complexType>
</element>
```

3.2.2   SIMPLE TYPES

An element is defined as a simple type if it does not contain child elements or attributes. By default, an attribute is a simple type; after all, it can contain only one value. If you consider DTD rules, the simple type would be used when defining an element to contain only parsed character data. Simple types are based on built-in datatypes, which are defined by the W3C document *XML Schema Part 2: Datatypes*. We cover them later in the "Declaring Elements" section.

Schema Terms

The following are some terms that you should be familiar with when reading through the following sections:

- *Definition.* Defines a complex or simple type that either contains element or attribute declarations or references element or attribute declarations defined elsewhere in the document.

- *Declaration.* Defines an element or attribute name and datatype.

- *Global.* An element or attribute declared under the schema element rather than as a part of a complex-type definition. This means that the element or attribute declaration will be an immediate child of the schema element. After you have declared the element and/or attribute under the schema element, you can reference them in other definitions (using a ref attribute).

- *Local.* An element or attribute declared as a child of any element other than the schema element. The term *local* is not used often, but it helps define the distinction between the two. We use the term *local* throughout this chapter.

3.3   Schema for Structures

The W3C *XML Schema Part 1: Structures* document defines the schema vocabulary. Because the XML Schema standard is an XML vocabulary, it uses elements and attributes. The following sections cover the use of many of the XML Schema elements and attributes defined by the structures document.

3.3.1   DECLARING ELEMENTS

One of the easiest ways to understand how to declare an element in XML Schema; is to see it in action. Remembering back to the rules of DTDs outlined in Chapter 2, you would use the following DTD syntax to declare a song element with three child elements: title, artist, and fileSize.

```
<!ELEMENT song (title, artist, fileSize)>
<!ELEMENT title (#PCDATA)>
<!ELEMENT artist (#PCDATA)>
<!ELEMENT fileSize (#PCDATA)>
```

Now, take a look at the schema equivalent:

```
<schema xmlns="http://www.w3.org/2001/XMLSchema"
        xmlns:song="http://www.lanw.com/namespaces/song"
        targetNamespace="http://www.lanw.com/namespaces/
        song">
<element name="song">
    <complexType>
        <sequence>
            <element ref="song:title"/>
            <element ref="song:artist"/>
            <element ref="song:fileSize"/>
        </sequence>
    </complexType>
</element>
<element name="title" type="string"/>
<element name="artist" type="string"/>
<element name="fileSize" type="string"/>
</schema>
```

You also should notice that schema is the root element (also known as the *document element*). It requires a namespace declaration that points to the schema namespace. In this case, it is defined as a default namespace; therefore, it does not need the xsd prefix. This means that all elements that do not use a prefix belong to the schema namespace.

In addition, there is also a namespace for our song elements, which will be prefixed with song:. This allows you to refer to elements that are already declared. This becomes more obvious shortly.

The third and final defined namespace is known as a target namespace. A *target namespace* defines the namespace of elements that can be validated by the schema (this means all the elements in the XML document).

As with our DTD example, the schema document has four element type declarations. The first declaration is defined as follows:

```
<element name="song">
    <complexType>
        <sequence>
```

```
            <element ref="song:title"/>
            <element ref="song:artist"/>
            <element ref="song:fileSize"/>
        </sequence>
    </complexType>
</element>
```

The `element` element (yes, that's right) declares an element. The `name` attribute names the element. In this case, the element is named `song`. The next step is to identify the element as a `complexType` because it contains other elements. Therefore, the `complexType` element is added.

Now it is time to deal with content models. XML Schema allows you to define several different types of content models—all using different schema elements and attributes. For example, most of the following elements (also called *compositors*) can translate to DTD equivalents:

- `all`. No DTD equivalent.
- `any`. Similar to the `ANY` keyword.
- `choice`. Similar to the pipe bar (|) connector.
- `group`. No DTD equivalent.
- `sequence`. Similar to the comma (,) connector.

There are a few attributes that can be used to define content models as well:

- `minOccurs="value"`. Similar to the DTD occurrence indicators (?, +, and *).
- `maxOccurs="value"`. Similar to the DTD occurrence indicators (?, +, and *).

We look at each of these in this chapter. For our example, we focus on the `sequence` element.

The `sequence` element defines an ordered sequence for allowable child elements. For example, the following snippet requires that the child elements appear in order of `title`, `artist`, and `fileSize`:

```
<sequence>
    <element ref="song:title"/>
    <element ref="song:artist"/>
    <element ref="song:fileSize"/>
</sequence>
```

Next, the child elements are defined. There are two ways to use the `element` element: as a definition and as a reference. In this case it is used as a reference. First, the element references are nested, so you know that they are children of the `song` element. You know that the element's `title`, `artist`, and `fileSize` will be defined later because the `ref` attribute references later-defined element declarations.

Now what about that `song` prefix? Well, after you declare an element within the scope of a `targetNamespace`, you must reference it as part of that namespace, no matter where you use it. In this case you reference the element as part of the `ref` attribute, so you must use the namespace prefix.

Take a second to look back at the namespace definitions:

```
<schema xmlns="http://www.w3.org/2001/XMLSchema"
        xmlns:song="http://www.lanw.com/namespaces/song"
        targetNamespace="http://www.lanw.com/namespaces/
        song">
```

Remember that the first namespace is the default namespace for schema elements. This means that if you use (or reference) any nonschema elements, they must be defined with an alternative prefix. The last two namespaces work together. The last one (`targetNamespace`) defines a namespace to be associated with all declared elements. This is not an `xmlns` namespace definition; this simply states that if these elements are used in a document, they must belong to the defined namespace. Because of this, the second namespace (`xmlns:song`) is included to do just that: define the appropriate namespace for the elements just in case you need to use them. And indeed you do.

So here is what has been covered so far:

```
<schema xmlns="http://www.w3.org/2001/XMLSchema"
    xmlns:song="http://www.lanw.com/namespaces/song"
    targetNamespace="http://www.lanw.com/namespaces/song">
<element name="song">
    <complexType>
        <sequence>
            <element ref="song:title"/>
            <element ref="song:artist"/>
            <element ref="song:fileSize"/>
        </sequence>
    </complexType>
</element>
<element name="title" type="string"/>
<element name="artist" type="string"/>
<element name="fileSize" type="string"/>
</schema>
```

All that is left is to define each child element. Because each element should contain only character data, it is defined to conform to a string datatype. The `name` attribute names the element, and the `type` attribute defines its datatype. This is where schemas can get interesting because, unlike DTDs, you can define datatypes for your elements as well as your attributes.

MAKING CHOICES

In the preceding example you defined three child elements that were required to occur in a specific sequence. Now you want to allow the author a choice between three elements. The DTD equivalent is

```
<!ELEMENT song (title | artist | fileSize)>
```

This DTD snippet requires that the document author make a choice between the three child elements. The XML Schema equivalent is

```
<schema xmlns="http://www.w3.org/2001/XMLSchema"
       xmlns:song="http://www.lanw.com/namespaces/song"
       targetNamespace="http://www.lanw.com/namespaces/
       song">
<element name="song">
   <complexType>
      <choice>
         <element ref="song:title"/>
         <element ref="song:artist"/>
         <element ref="song:fileSize"/>
      </choice>
   </complexType>
</element>
<element name="title" type="string"/>
<element name="artist" type="string"/>
<element name="fileSize" type="string"/>
</schema>
```

The only thing that changed from the first example was that the `sequence` element changed to the `choice` element. Now the document author chooses just one of the child elements.

DEFINING OCCURRENCES

Next, you can further augment the choice example and allow for multiple choices. The DTD equivalent would be

```
<!ELEMENT song (title | artist | fileSize)*>
```

Notice that the only thing added was an asterisk (*) to the end of the content model. This allows multiple choices to be made. In an XML Schema document, this is done using the following markup (notice the `minOccurs` and `maxOccurs` attributes):

```
<schema xmlns="http://www.w3.org/2001/XMLSchema"
       xmlns:song="http://www.lanw.com/namespaces/song"
       targetNamespace="http://www.lanw.com/namespaces/
       song">
<element name="song">
   <complexType>
      <choice minOccurs="1" maxOccurs="unbounded">
         <element ref="song:title"/>
         <element ref="song:artist"/>
         <element ref="song:fileSize"/>
      </choice>
```

```
      </complexType>
</element>
<element name="title" type="string"/>
<element name="artist" type="string"/>
<element name="fileSize" type="string"/>
</schema>
```

This markup also includes two additional attributes:

- `minOccurs="nonNegativeInteger"`. This defines the minimum number of occurrences. The default value is 1, so if you leave out the attribute, it is assumed that the choice is required.

- `maxOccurs="nonNegativeInteger | unbounded"`. This defines the maximum number of occurrences. The value can be a number or the keyword unbounded. The unbounded value is equal to using the asterisk (*) in a DTD content model and therefore places no limit on the number of occurrences. The default value is 1, so if you leave out this attribute, it is assumed that the choice may occur only once.

These attributes also may be used with the `element` element to define the number of times a given element may occur. For example, you could add the following to your markup to allow the artist's name to occur up to five times:

```
<schema xmlns="http://www.w3.org/2001/XMLSchema"
        xmlns:song="http://www.lanw.com/namespaces/song"
        targetNamespace="http://www.lanw.com/namespaces/
        song">
<element name="song">
    <complexType>
        <choice minOccurs="1" maxOccurs="unbounded">
            <element ref="song:title"/>
            <element ref="song:artist" maxOccurs="5"/>
            <element ref="song:fileSize"/>
        </choice>
    </complexType>
</element>
<element name="title" type="string"/>
<element name="artist" type="string"/>
<element name="fileSize" type="string"/>
</schema>
```

ALLOWING RANDOMNESS

You can allow for the three child elements to occur in any order using the `all` element. For example:

```
<schema xmlns="http://www.w3.org/2001/XMLSchema"
        xmlns:song="http://www.lanw.com/namespaces/song"
```

```
        targetNamespace="http://www.lanw.com/namespaces/
        song">
<element name="song">
    <complexType>
        <all>
            <element ref="song:title"/>
            <element ref="song:artist"/>
            <element ref="song:fileSize"/>
        </all>
    </complexType>
</element>
<element name="title" type="string"/>
<element name="artist" type="string"/>
<element name="fileSize" type="string"/>
</schema>
```

Because the `minOccurs` and `maxOccurs` attributes are not used, the default value is assumed, and therefore, the document author is required to use each child element once. However, the order is up to the document author. There are no unique attributes for this element.

MIXING AND MATCHING

In this section you look at several of these options rolled into one example:

```
<schema xmlns="http://www.w3.org/2001/XMLSchema"
        xmlns:song="http://www.lanw.com/namespaces/song"
        targetNamespace="http://www.lanw.com/namespaces/
        song">
<element name="song">
    <complexType>
        <sequence>
            <choice>
                <element ref="song:title"/>
                <element ref="song:artist"/>
            </choice>
                <element ref="song:fileSize"/>
        </sequence>
    </complexType>
</element>
<element name="title" type="string"/>
<element name="artist" type="string"/>
<element name="fileSize" type="string"/>
</schema>
```

In this example you first use the `sequence` element to define the order in which the elements must occur. Next, you use the `choice` element to define a choice for the first child element. After the closing `choice` tag, you define the last child element.

You should come up with something similar to the following document:

```
<song xmlns="http://www.lanw.com/namespaces/song">
    <title>text of title</title>
    <fileSize>text of fileSize</fileSize>
</song>
```

Or

```
<song xmlns="http://www.lanw.com/namespaces/song">
    <artist>text of artist</artist>
    <fileSize>text of fileSize</fileSize>
</song>
```

There are only two options for our document. First, both options require that the song element is the root element. Next, you know that the song element must have only two child elements. For the first child element, you have a choice: title or artist. For the next child element, you must use fileSize. Because you don't use the minOccurs or maxOccurs attribute for any of the definitions or declarations, you can only use each element once.

3.3.2 DECLARING ATTRIBUTES

Declaring attributes is much like declaring elements. For attribute declarations, you use the attribute element. Suppose that you want to add a genre attribute to the song element. The DTD syntax would be as follows:

```
<!ELEMENT song (title, artist, fileSize)>
<!ATTLIST song genre CDATA #REQUIRED>
```

Now take a look at the XML Schema equivalent:

```
<schema xmlns="http://www.w3.org/2001/XMLSchema"
        xmlns:song="http://www.lanw.com/namespaces/song"
        targetNamespace="http://www.lanw.com/namespaces/
        song">
<element name="song">
    <complexType>
        <sequence>
            <element ref="song:title"/>
            <element ref="song:artist"/>
            <element ref="song:fileSize"/>
        </sequence>
        <attribute name="genre" type="string"
            use="required"/>
    </complexType>
</element>
<element name="title" type="string"/>
<element name="artist" type="string"/>
```

```
<element name="fileSize" type="string"/>
</schema>
```

In this example you define the `genre` attribute, which is required and can take any character data as its value. The most common attributes used with the `attribute` element are

- `name="name"`. This defines the name for the attribute.
- `ref="name"`. This is used to reference global attribute declarations. Global declarations are elements or attributes defined as children of the `schema` element and referenced later. Note that global declarations cannot contain references.
- `type="name"`. This defines the datatype for the attribute.
- `use="prohibited | optional | required | default | fixed"`. This is used to indicate whether the attribute is required or optional. You also may declare the attribute to contain a fixed or default value. In this case you must define the fixed or default value with the `value` attribute. The default value is `optional`.
- `value="string"`. This defines the fixed or default value. It is used in conjunction with the `use` attribute.

You also can define the attribute to have a default value, as in the following:

```
<schema xmlns="http://www.w3.org/2001/XMLSchema"
        xmlns:song="http://www.lanw.com/namespaces/song"
        targetNamespace="http://www.lanw.com/namespaces/
        song">
<element name="song">
    <complexType>
        <sequence>
            <element ref="song:title"/>
            <element ref="song:artist"/>
            <element ref="song:fileSize"/>
        </sequence>
        <attribute name="genre" type="string"
        use="default" value="unknown"/>
    </complexType>
</element>
<element name="title" type="string"/>
<element name="artist" type="string"/>
<element name="fileSize" type="string"/>
</schema>
```

Or, for example, you may want to create a new attribute that will identify the Uniform Resource Identifier (URI) where the song can be downloaded:

```
<schema xmlns="http://www.w3.org/2001/XMLSchema"
        xmlns:song="http://www.lanw.com/namespaces/song"
```

```
        targetNamespace="
        http://www.lanw.com/namespaces/song">
<element name="song">
    <complexType>
        <sequence>
            <element ref="song:title"/>
            <element ref="song:artist"/>
            <element ref="song:fileSize"/>
        </sequence>
        <attribute name="genre" type="string"
        use="default"
        value="unknown"/>
        <attribute name="href" type="uriReference"
        use="required"/>
    </complexType>
</element>
<element name="title" type="string"/>
<element name="artist" type="string"/>
<element name="fileSize" type="string"/>
</schema>
```

Our new addition is a required attribute named `href` and can accept a `uriReference` datatype. The `uriReference` and `string` datatypes are the only two datatypes that we discuss; however, there are several to choose from, and you can create your own. All of this is covered in the following section.

3.4   Schema for Datatypes

One of the main drawbacks to using DTDs is that they do not allow for sophisticated datatyping. Take a second to refresh your memory:

- *Attribute datatypes:* ID, IDREF(S), CDATA, NOTATION, ENTITY, ENTITIES, NMTOKEN(S), and enumerated values
- *Element datatypes:* PCDATA and/or child elements

And that is it. One of the reasons schemas have become so attractive is that they allow for more sophisticated datatyping. Wouldn't it be nice to require the ISBN number to contain exactly 10 digits? When it comes time to validate your documents, you can be sure that there are no entry mistakes. What about dates? Would it be helpful to define a naming convention for dates? XML Schema datatyping is defined by the *XML Schema Part 2: Datatypes* document.

Take a second to look at a DTD fragment:

```
<!ATTLIST book price CDATA #IMPLIED>
```

With this declaration, you, as the document author, are free to use any character data string as the value; for example, the following would be valid:

```
<book price="silly">
<book price="22">
<book price=".">
```

If you use XML Schema, however, you can define the value as a decimal value. For example:

```
<attribute name="price" type="decimal"/>
```

Therefore, only a decimal number such as the following would be acceptable:

```
<book price="22.22">
```

Just what can you do with datatypes? The specification categorizes datatypes in several different dichotomies:

- *Primitive versus derived.* Primitive datatypes are not defined in terms of other datatypes, whereas derived datatypes are defined in terms of other datatypes.

- *Atomic versus list versus union.* Atomic datatypes are those with values that are regarded by the specification as being indivisible. List datatypes are defined as those with values that consist of a finite-length sequence of values of an atomic datatype. And finally, union datatypes are those in which value spaces and lexical spaces are the union of the value spaces and lexical spaces of two or more datatypes.

- *Built-in versus user-derived.* Built-in datatypes are those which are defined by the specification (they can be both derived and primitive). User-derived datatypes are derived datatypes that are defined by schema designers (like you).

In this section you find out about built-in datatypes. For more information on datatypes, see the XML Schema Datatype specification (www.w3.org/TR/xmlschema-2/).

3.4.1   BUILT-IN DATATYPES

There are two different types of built-in datatypes: primitive and derived. *Primitive datatypes* are the foundation for all other datatypes. *Derived datatypes* are based on (built from) the primitive datatypes. We look at primitive datatypes first.

PRIMITIVE DATATYPES

Table 3-1 defines all primitive datatypes.

Table 3-1   XML Schema Primitive Datatypes

Datatype	Example Value
string	Hello World
boolean	{true, false}

float	12.56E3, 12, 12560, 0, -0, INF, -INF, NAN
double	12.56E3, 12, 12560, 0, -0, INF, -INF, NAN
decimal	7.08
duration	P0Y1347M
dateTime	1999-05-31T13:20:00-05:00
time	13:20:00-05:00
date	2001-07-29
gYearMonth	2001-07
gYear	2001
gMonthDay	07-29
gDay	29
gMonth	07
hexBinary	0FB7
base64Binary	bW9t
anyURI	http://www.lanw.com
QName	mc:song
NOTATION	*notation*

DERIVED DATATYPES

The following are the derived datatypes defined by the datatypes document:

```
normalizedString
token
language
ID
IDREF
IDREFS
ENTITY
ENTITIES
NMTOKEN
NMTOKENS
```

```
Name
NCName
integer
nonPositiveInteger
negativeInteger
long
int
short
byte
nonNegativeInteger
unsignedLong
unsignedInt
unsignedShort
unsignedByte
positiveInteger
```

 Review Questions

3.1 XML Schema was created by the W3C as an alternative for which of the following?
   a. RELAX
   b. Schematron
   c. DTD
   d. XDR

3.2 Which of the following is *not* true about XML Schema?
   a. It allows users to define patterns for their own datatypes.
   b. It is namespace aware.
   c. It allows for complex datatyping.
   d. It is defined in one specification document.

3.3 XML Schema defines an equivalent for DTD general entities.
   a. True
   b. False

3.4 Which of the following is a complete element declaration?
   a. `<element name="contact" type="string">`
   b. `<element name="contact">`
   c. `<element type="string" name="contact"/>`
   d. `<element type="string">`

3.5 Which of the following is an incomplete attribute declaration?
   a. `<attribute name="isbn" type="isbnType"/>`
   b. `<attribute name="isbn" type="integer"/>`
   c. `<attribute ref="contactID"/>`
   d. `<attribute name="contactID"/>`

3.6 Which of the following attribute combinations in the element declarations requires that the `contact` element occurs at least once and may repeat five times?

   a. `<element name="contact" type="string" minOccurs="1" maxOccurs= "5"/>`

   b. `<element name="contact" type="string" minoccurs="1" maxoccurs= "5"/>`

   c. `<element name="contact" type="string" maxOccurs="1" minOccurs= "5"/>`

   d. `<element name="contact" type="string" maxOccurs="5"/>`

3.7 Of the following, which is not a type of datatype defined by XML Schema?

   a. Derived

   b. Combined

   c. Primitive

   d. Atomic

3.8 Which of the following does not use the `string` datatype properly?

   a. `<element name="name" type="string"/>`

   b. `<attribute name="name" type="string"/>`

   c. `<complexType name="name" type="string"/>`

   d. `<restriction base="string">`

3.9 Which of the following is a correct usage of the `dateTime` datatype?

   a. `1999-05-31T13:20:00-05:00`

   b. `1999-T05-31-13:20:00-05:00`

   c. `1999-31T13:20:00-05:00`

   d. `1999-05-31T13:20:00`

3.10 Which of the following is not a primitive datatype?

   a. `integer`

   b. `duration`

   c. `gYear`

   d. `boolean`

Problems

3.1 Define a declaration for a `contact` element that contains `name` and `email` children elements. The `name` and `email` elements must occur only once and must occur in the order of `name` followed by `email`.

3.2 Add an attribute declaration to the `contact` element. The attribute should be an `ID` datatype with the name `id`.

3.3 Declare a `complexType` definition with the name `contactType` that allows for the same content model as the `contact` element in Problem 3.1.

3.4 Define an attribute declaration that references the `complexType` definition. Name the new element `customer`.

3.5 Create an attribute declaration that would be the equivalent to the following DTD attribute list declaration: `<!ATTLIST book cat NMTOKENS #REQUIRED>`. You do not need to define the accompanying `book` element declaration, only the attribute declaration.

Answers to Review Questions

3.1 c. XML Schema was created as an alternative for XML 1.0 DTDs.

3.2 d. XML Schema is defined by two specification documents: XML Schema Part 1: Structures and XML Schema Part 2: Datatypes.

3.3 b. False. XML Schema does not define equivalents for DTD general entities.

3.4 c. The following complete element declaration allows for a `contact` element that can only contain a string datatype: `<element type="string" name="contact"/>`.

3.5 d. Attribute declarations can reference either predefined attribute declarations or both the name and type must be defined.

3.6 a. The `maxOccurs` attribute defines the maximum number of occurrences, whereas the `minOccurs` attribute defines the minimum number of occurrences for an element.

3.7 b. Derived, primitive, and atomic are types of datatypes defined by the XML Schema specification.

3.8 c. The `complexType` element cannot contain a `type` attribute that is used to define a datatype.

3.9 a. `1999-05-31T13:20:00-05:00` is the correct use of the `dateTime` datatype.

3.10 a. `integer` is a derived datatype.

Solutions to Problems

3.1
```
<element name="contact">
    <complexType>
        <sequence>
            <element name="name" type="string"/>
            <element name="email" type="string"/>
        </sequence>
    </complexType>
</element>
```
3.2
```
<element name="contact">
    <complexType>
        <sequence>
            <element name="name" type="string"/>
            <element name="email" type="string"/>
        </sequence>
        <attribute name="id" type="ID"/>
    </complexType>
</element>
```
3.3
```
<complexType name="contactType">
    <sequence>
        <element name="name" type="string"/>
        <element name="email" type="string"/>
    </sequence>
</complexType>
```
3.4
```
<element name="customer" ref="contactType"/>
```
3.5
```
<attribute name="cat" type="NMTOKENS" use="required"/>
```

CHAPTER 4

Cascading Style Sheets

4.1   CSS in Browsers and Components

Cascading Style Sheets (CSS) allow the Extensible Markup Language (XML) author to present a document in an attractive fashion and indicate to the browser (or other user agent) the style properties to be applied to components of the XML document. As you may recall from previous chapters, the tags used in XML, although they may appear to be very much like Hypertext Markup Language (HTML) tags, offer no indication of intended presentation markup. Remember that XML is *content-driven* as opposed to *presentation-driven*. You can solve this dilemma very easily by using a CSS style sheet with the XML document.

There are various methods that you can use, and we touch on several of the most common in this chapter. Also, bear in mind that as of this writing, CSS2 has been established as the current recommendation by the World Wide Web Consortium (W3C), with CSS3 already in the works. For this book and its examples, we focus on and use CSS2. The complete CSS2 specification (and any updates) can be found at `http://www.w3.org/TR/CSS2/`.

One big issue, and hopefully one that will calm down a bit, is the issue of browser compatibility. The main players in the browser wars are Microsoft Internet Explorer 5.5+ and Netscape Navigator 6.0+. In addition, there are a couple of other browsers that should be considered for their strong XML and CSS support: Opera 5 and the Amaya browser. All these browsers offer a mixed and varied bag of native XML support, but by incorporating CSS, they all have a greater success in presenting XML. We assume that browsers will continue to evolve *toward* the specifications as opposed to *away* from them, and our examples are based on the current crop of user agents just mentioned.

Before you can apply CSS to XML, we should address some of the terms and concepts used to create style sheets. A CSS style sheet provides additional (and, in the case of XML,) all presentation information for the documents to which it is applied. This information is based on the elements or class of elements used in the content of the document. Most (if not all) of the CSS concepts apply to HTML and the Extensible Hypertext Markup Language (XHTML) as well as to XML.

Here are a few of the basic terms from the W3C standard with which you should be familiar:

- *Style sheet*. A style sheet consists of additional markup in the form of statements that govern *presentation* of the document. Style sheets generally are one of three basic types (which provide the cascade): *author*, *user*, or *user agent*. The first of these, the *author* style, is presentation specified by the author of the document or the software used to create the document. This style may be overwritten (or superseded) by the *user* style, which is the style the user has set for his or her particular needs, whether by preference or because of special needs. Finally, there is the style dictated by the *user agent,* which is the style sheet that typically takes precedence over the preceding two types of style markup and often is a limitation brought about by the browser or another user agent. In practice, the document author provides values for each attribute, allowing them to *cascade* down to the defaults of the browser or software.

- *Valid style sheet*. Like XML itself, CSS should validate to the accepted standards indicated for the level of CSS used. Luckily, any CSS1 documents should validate against CSS2, but for critical applications, these should be updated to current standards. As part of the validation process, the style sheet will be checked for uses of rules, property names, and property values defined in the CSS specification.

- *Source document*. The *source document* is the document to which (one or more) style sheets refer. This is encoded in a language that represents the document as a tree of elements. Each element consists of a name that identifies the type of element and, optionally, a number of attributes.

- *Document language*. This is the encoding language used in the source document, for example, XML, XHTML, or HTML.

- *Element*. This is the familiar element as used in Standard Generalized Markup Language (SGML), XML, HTML, and XHTML. This is the primary syntactic construct of the document language. Many CSS style sheet rules use the names of elements such as `br`, `table`, and `ul` (from HTML) to specify rendering information for them.

- *Attribute*. This is used with an element in the same way as an attribute-value pair. The value must be quoted. Single or double quotes are both acceptable. We just suggest that you be consistent in your usage.

- *Content*. This is the content associated with an element in the source document; not all elements have content, in which case they are called *empty elements*. The content of an element may include text. In addition, it can include a number of subelements, in which case the element is called the *parent* of those subelements.

- *Rendered content*. This is the content of an element after the rendering of the CSS style sheets has been applied. Rendered content also may be alternate text for an element (for example, the value of the HTML `alt` attribute) and may include items inserted implicitly or explicitly by the style sheet, such as bullets, numbering, and so on. The rendered content of a replaced element comes from outside the source document.

- *Document tree*. This is the tree of elements encoded in the source document. Each element in this tree has exactly one *parent,* with the exception of the root element, which has none.

- *Child*. Element A is called the *child* of element B if and only if element B is the *parent* of element A.

- *Descendant*. Element A is called a *descendant* of element B if either element A is a *child* of element B or element A is the *child* of element C that is a *descendant* of element B.

- *Ancestor*. Element A is called an *ancestor* of element B if and only if element B is a *descendant* of element A.

- *Sibling*. Element A is called a *sibling* of element B if and only if elements B and A share the same *parent* element. Element A is a *preceding sibling* if it comes *before* element B in the document tree. Element B is a *following sibling* if it comes *after* element B in the document tree.

A *CSS rule* generally consists of four parts: selectors, declarations, properties, and values. A *selector* is any element that you use to select where the style should be applied, for example p (in HTML). A *declaration* is the style itself, (e.g., `color: green`). The declaration is made up of two parts: the *property* (`color`) and the *value* (`green`). Notice that the syntax is slightly different from that of an attribute-value pair in HTML. In CSS, the property and the value are separated with a colon, which delimits the attribute from the value. All property declarations end with a semicolon, for example, p `{color: green; font-family: Arial}`.

Finally, there are two levels of declaring styles: *in-line* and *block*. In-line does *not* cause a line break when it is applied, whereas block inserts a leading line break. The two are discussed at length in the next section.

Styles often are declared in a separate file and given a `.css` extension. The CSS file is then referenced via a processing instruction (PI) in the XML document, for example:

```
<?xml:stylesheet href="example.css" type="text/css"?>
```

The same path/Uniform Resource Identifier (URI) rules apply to CSS files as to Document Type Definition (DTD) or other included files.

4.2   The display: block Property

The `display: block` property is very similar to and reminiscent of the results given by the paragraph (p) element in HTML. A *block* of text is assigned a style as an aggregate, with a preceding line break applied. The `display: block` property can contain styles of the `display: inline` variety without incurring a line break. For example, you may want to apply a font style to a block of text and then emphasize a portion of that text by setting a heavier font weight without breaking the flow of the text. For this example we'll use the `text` element for the body of text and the `author` element for the author's name, which is the emphasized portion.

We would declare our desired styles as

```
text {display: block}
author {display: inline;
      font-weight: bold}
```

Each declaration of a style is surrounded by braces (that is, { }). Each property declaration is separated by a semicolon (;), and more than one can occur in the style declaration. In addition, alternate values can be included, separated by a comma (,).

In our example, we indicate a simple `display: block` for the data contained in the `text` element, with no style applied other than the line break at the beginning of the rendered text. This behaves just like a standard p element in HTML. For the portion of the text contained in `author` element, we apply a `font-weight: bold`, with no line breaks. The full markup looks like this:

```
<?xml:stylesheet href="example.css" type="text/css"?>
<text>
For the duration of the semester we will focus on three authors,
      specifically
   <author>John Steinbeck</author>,
   <author>Ernest Hemingway</author>, and
   <author>J.D. Salinger</author>.

Each of these three will be discussed in turn.
</text>
```

Figure 4-1 shows this markup rendered with CSS. As you see in this example, the data between the `author` tags appears without line breaks, as per our CSS declarations. Even though CSS declarations will grow in length and complexity, the rules remain the same, as you'll see in further examples.

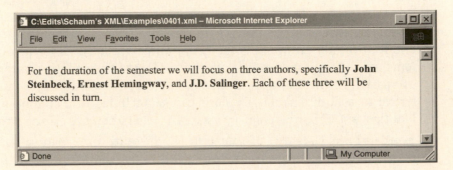

Fig. 4-1. XML rendered with CSS.

In addition, you should keep in mind that all these examples are based simply on CSS. Another way to apply style is through the *Extensible Stylesheet Language*

(XSL), which is covered thoroughly in Chapter 7. XSL is made up of three sub-components (as defined by the W3C):

- *XPath*. XML Path Language, a language for referencing specific parts of an XML document.
- *XSLT*. XSL Transformations, a language for describing how to transform one XML document (represented as a tree) into another.
- *XSL*. Extensible Stylesheet Language, which is XSLT plus a description of a set of formatting objects and formatting properties.

4.3   Fonts

One of the most common uses of CSS is in rendering fonts. Because the browser is still the user agent of choice for most XML documents, the selection of font style, size, weight, and so on is of great importance to the design of the CSS document. Most of the styles that are applied to fonts are intended to accomplish two goals: One is for design and visual appeal, whereas the other is for readability and emphasis.

The font style *properties* are familiar to most HTML authors. CSS1 provides these basic font properties:

- `color`. Either as a color name (for example, `red`) or a red-green-blue (RGB) value (for example, `255,0,0`). If you choose to use a color name, be aware that browsers may render the colors differently. You are better off using the RGB values whenever possible.
- `font-weight`. Either as a keyword (`bold`, `normal`, etc.) or as a numerical value (`100` through `900`). The keywords allow `bolder` and `lighter`, with each application changing the numerical value by 100. For example, `normal` equates to `400`, and `bold` is the same as `700`.
- `font-family`. Use as a family name (`Arial`, `Courier`, etc.) or generic (`serif`, `sans-serif`, etc.). For cross-platform documents, use of the generic font-family grouping is the better choice because different operating systems use different names for very similar fonts. The generic groups are defined as `serif`, `sans-serif`, `cursive`, `fantasy`, and `monospace`. As an alternative to a family name, a generic can be included in a comma-separated list like this: h4 { font-family: Arial, Helvetica, sans-serif }
- `font-size`. Uses one of four criteria: absolute size, relative size, length, or percentage. The absolute-size keywords are defined as `xx-small`, `x-small`, `small`, `medium`, `large`, `x-large`, and `xx-large`. Relative sizes are `larger` and `smaller`, each of which changes the absolute sizes in the direction indicated. Length and percentage values should not take the font-size table into account when calculating the font-size of the element. Negative values are not allowed.

- `font-style`. Selects between `normal`, `italic`, or `oblique`. The `normal` selection is an upright style, and `italic` and `oblique` refer to their respective counterparts, when available within a font family.

- `text-decoration`. Adds `none`, `underline`, `overline`, `line-through`, or `blink`. If you want text to `blink`, here's your chance. The other decoration properties allow line-through effects, overlines, or an underline. If `none` is specified, text that normally would be underlined is not, for example, the anchor (a) element in HTML.

- `text-transform`. Sets `capitalize`, `uppercase`, `lowercase`, or `none`. The `capitalize` selection sets the first letter of the word as an uppercase character; `uppercase` and `lowercase` set the case of the entire word.

CSS2 adds the following font properties:

- `text-shadow`. Allows the creation of a shadow effect on text by specifying a shadow offset (horizontal and vertical) and optionally may specify a blur radius and a shadow color. For example:

```
h3 { text-shadow: 3px 4px 5px red }
```

This creates a red shadow offset 3 pixels to the right with 4 pixels below and a 5-pixel blur. Positive values for offset are *right* and *below*.

- `font-size-adjust`. Specifies a desired aspect value for a replacement font to maintain legibility as the size of the font decreases. The larger the `font-size-adjust` value, the more legible the font will be when reduced in size. For example, the popular font Verdana has an aspect value of 0.58; when Verdana's font size is 100 units, its *x* height is 58 units. For comparison, Times New Roman has an aspect value of 0.46. Verdana therefore will tend to remain more legible at smaller sizes than Times New Roman. Conversely, Verdana often will look too big if substituted for Times New Roman at a chosen size. As a result, Verdana will be sized slightly smaller to maintain its relative legibility.

- `font-stretch`. Selects a normal, condensed, or expanded face from a font family. This is specified by an absolute or relative keyword. Absolute keyword values have the following order, from narrowest to widest: `ultra-condensed`, `extra-condensed`, `condensed`, `semi-condensed`, `normal`, `semi-expanded`, `expanded`, `extra-expanded`, and `ultra-expanded`. The relative keyword `wider` sets the value to the next expanded value above the inherited value but not increasing it above `ultra-expanded`. The relative keyword `narrower` sets the value to the next condensed value below the inherited value but not decreasing it below `ultra-condensed`.

In practice, font properties often are combined in one declaration. For example, the declaration

```
author { display: inline;
        font-weight: bold }
```

can be supplemented with a font color by adding the property statement `color: green` to the declaration, which then becomes

```
author { display: inline;
         font-weight: bold;
         color: green }
```

Multiple properties can be specified in this way as long as they share a common element and make logical sense. As with a DTD, creating shared CSS files is a good way to ensure consistency between multiple XML documents. As always, pay close attention to the syntax, completeness, and therefore validity of your CSS style sheets.

4.4   Text Alignment

The `text-align` property describes how the designer intends the text to be positioned, aligned, and justified within the browser window. Unfortunately, many of the values specified are still left wide open to interpretation by the user agent; therefore, somewhat unpredictable results can occur. Hopefully, the migration to W3C-recommended standards will reduce the potential for error, but for now, it is still wise to view documents in as many applications as possible, with an eye to reducing presentation errors before publishing them.

The common uses for text alignment are `left`, `right`, `center`, and `justify` (or string). When used in conjunction with the `display: block` property, it is easy to create CSS declarations that allow the presentation to achieve the desired results. Because `text-align` inherits properties, it lends itself to use with the `div` element or other high-level text formatting elements.

Here are some examples of the use of the `text-align` property:

```
div.center { text-align: center }
div.left { text-align: left }
```

For table cells only, you can use a string to specify to which string the table cells will align. This is useful for creating columnar lists in which a particular string or character is repeated and may be used to align the text. One of the most obvious examples would be a list of expenses, where the dollar sign ($) and period (.) are used for alignment. This technique will work best if text fits on one line.

4.5   Borders

CSS is intended to allow developers to dress up documents for improved readability as well as aesthetics. The `border` property is made up of `border-width`, `border-style`, and `border-color`. Each of these consists of subproperties and attributes.

The `border-width` property is a shorthand property for setting `border-width-top`, `border-width-right`, `border-width-bottom`, and `border-width-left` at the same time in a style sheet. It is comprised of a list containing from one to four values, each of which maps to a specific aspect of the `border-width`.

A precedence from the W3C is

- *One value*. All four border widths are set to this value. For example, all four borders in this example are set to thin:

  `h1 { border-width: thin }`

- *Two values*. Top and bottom border widths are set to the first value, and right and left border widths are set to the second. Here we have the top border as thin and the bottom as `thick`:

  `h1 { border-width: thin thick }`

- *Three values*. The top border is set to the first value, the right and left borders are set to the second value, and bottom border is set to the third value. In this example, the top border is `thin`, the right and left borders are `thick`, and the bottom is `medium`:

  `h1 { border-width: thin thick medium }`

- *Four values*. This sets the top, right, bottom, and left borders, respectively. In this example, the top border is `thin`, the right border is `thick`, the left border is `medium`, and the bottom border is `thin`. The acceptable values for `border-width` are `thin`, `medium`, `thick`, or a `length` value, as long as the value is not a negative number:

  `h1 { border-width: thin thick medium thin }`

Border color is specified like `border-width` and refers to sides. The same order is followed, and one to four values may be indicated, or each `border-color` may be specified using `border-left` (or `right`, `top`, or `bottom`) as it is for `width` and `style`. The color is set using either a color name or an RGB value.

Border style also may be set using position (`left`, `right`, `top`, or `bottom`) and one of the following eight styles: `dotted`, `dashed`, `solid`, `double`, `groove`, `ridge`, `inset`, `outset`, or `none`. The styles are described as follows:

- `dotted`. The border is a dotted line drawn on *top* of the background of the element.

- `dashed`. The border is a dotted line also drawn on *top* of the background of the element.

- `solid`. A border of a solid line.

- `double`. The border is a double line drawn on *top* of the background of the element. The sum of the two single lines and the space between equals the `border-width` value.

- groove. A three-dimensional groove is drawn in colors based on the color value.
- ridge. A three-dimensional ridge is drawn in colors based on the color value.
- inset. A three-dimensional inset is drawn in colors based on the color value.
- outset. A three-dimensional outset is drawn in colors based on the color value.

One thing to keep in mind with border-style, as well as with the other border properties, is that you are still dependent on the user agent when it comes to the final rendering of your chosen style, and therefore, testing is a good idea.

Putting all the border possibilities together, we can start to generate some interesting combinations from simple to quite elaborate (and possibly hideous).

If you specify just border, the border properties are set all the way around using the same values. For example, this places a solid red border on all four sides of a paragraph:

```
p { border: solid red }
```

This example does the same but with a lot more text:

```
p {
        border-top: solid red;
        border-right: solid red;
        border-bottom: solid red;
        border-left: solid red
}
```

However, if we modify the second example, we can then set four different border color, style, and size combinations:

```
p {
        border-top: dotted green thin;
        border-right: solid red thick;
        border-bottom: dashed blue medium;
        border-left: ridge yellow thin
}
```

4.6   Backgrounds

The use of backgrounds in CSS for XML is reminiscent of the HTML property of the same name. Like its HTML counterpart, background can be either a color or an image. Additionally, for the background image, its position, whether it is repeated or not, and if it is fixed relative to the foreground or if it scrolls can all be set. The default value for background is transparent, so any color applied to the parent will appear to be inherited by the child unless a value is set. The syntax for `background-color` is simple:

```
p { background-color: #F00F00 }
```

The color itself may be an RGB value or a color name (for example, `green`). Also keep in mind that we are applying the background as style, not as a `body` property like we would in HTML, so we can set apart different CSS elements very easily.

If you choose to use `background-image` either alone or in combination with `background-color`, you have a few more properties that you can set. The most obvious one would be the URI of the image you wish to use. As is always the case, you must follow the rules for specifying the file location, either via a path on the local server or by means of the fully qualified URI. It is also a good idea to specify a background color as a backup to the image just in case there are issues with the user agent displaying the image or other problems.

You also might indicate whether the image repeats and, if so, along which axis. The available values are `repeat` (both directions, tiling), `repeat-x` (horizontal), `repeat-y` (vertical), and `no-repeat`. The default value is `repeat`.

Here is an example of a background that will have both a color (`red`) and an image (`leafs.gif`) that repeats vertically (along the *y* axis):

```
body {
      background: red URL(leafs.gif);
      background-repeat: repeat-y;
}
```

If you want a simple tiling background image, you would simply state

```
body { background: red URL(leafs.gif);}
```

and the image would, by default, repeat in both the *x* and *y* directions.

Another background property attachment; `background-attachment`, determines whether a background image scrolls with the canvas or is attached and remains relatively motionless to the content. The default value is `scroll`.

If you add the `background-attachment` property to the earlier example, it becomes

```
body {
      background: red URL(leafs.gif);
      background-repeat: repeat-y;
      background-attachment: fixed
}
```

In this instance, the background image will remain stationary relative to the content being rendered.

Next, we have the `background-position` property, which is a little trickier than some of the properties discussed so far. There are several ways to express `background-position`. You have the customary `left`, `right`, and `center`, as well as `top`, `bottom`, and `center`. You also can position the image by a percentage of the browser width and height or a length (such as `cm`). The horizontal value is specified first, and combinations are allowed. The defaults are 0%, 0% (upper left).

The following examples are all legal position declarations:

- `top left` and `left top` are equivalent to `0% 0%`.
- `top`, `top center`, and `center top` are equivalent to `50% 0%`.
- `right top` and `top right` are equivalent to `100% 0%`.
- `left`, `left center`, and `center left` are equivalent to `0% 50%`.
- `center` and `center center` are equivalent to `50% 50%`.
- `right`, `right center`, and `center right` are equivalent to `100% 50%`.
- `bottom left` and `left bottom` are equivalent to `0% 100%`.
- `bottom`, `bottom center`, and `center bottom` are equivalent to `50% 100%`.
- `bottom right` and `right bottom` are equivalent to `100% 100%`

We will add to our example by placing the background image in its desired position:

```
body {
        background: red URL(leafs.gif);
        background-repeat: repeat-y;
        background-attachment: fixed;
        background-position: right top
    }
```

This places the image all the way to the right and at the top of the canvas. We also could declare

```
body {
        background: red URL(leafs.gif);
        background-repeat: repeat-y;
        background-attachment: fixed;
        background-position: 100% 0%
    }
```

and get the same result.

One more way of stating this might be a combination:

```
body {
        background: red URL(leafs.gif);
        background-repeat: repeat-y;
        background-attachment: fixed;
        background-position: 100% top
    }
```

4.7 Real-World Issues: Using CSS for XML Delivery

To include CSS (either CSS1 or CSS2 and beyond) in an XML document, you simply include a processing instruction (PI) in the XML document's prologue, such as

```
<?xml-stylesheet type="text/css" href="my_CSS.css"?>
```

This PI indicates that the document you are presenting should include a CSS file called my_CSS.css of the encoding type text/css that is in the same directory as the calling XML document. The usual rules for path/URI information apply.

Remember that it isn't the XML processor itself that will be handling the style sheets but rather a software application capable of rendering the XML elements according to the descriptions provided by the CSS rules defined in the PI. Whether you have one CSS rule set or have declared many, as long as the processor can locate a file of the same name as the one specified, you will be just fine (provided that the file contains the declarations you want to apply to the document).

A CSS file may be created in any text editor and then saved with an appropriate name and the file extension .css. As is the case for all markup, the editor of your choice should not add any non-American Standard Code for Information Interchange (ASCII) characters to your file. In other words, the cleaner, the better. Some of the XML editors listed in Chapter 1 will suffice as excellent CSS editors, as well as any simple ASCII text editor, such as HTML-Kit, EditPlus, or TextPad for the Windows platforms.

The basic rules that must be followed using CSS with XML are

- Embedded style sheets are not allowed.
- Styling as an attribute is not allowed.
- Linking is not allowed (for example, the link element in HTML).
- You need a PI:

  ```
  <?xml-stylesheet type="text/css" href="URL"?>
  ```

The use and application of CSS in XML involve authoring the XML document and the CSS style sheet, as well as associating the CSS style sheet with the XML document and rendering the XML document associated with the CSS style sheet. Authoring the XML document and the CSS are separate but very closely related processes. If you create a CSS file that is fairly comprehensive to your XML needs, then as you create XML documents, you simply need to associate them with the CSS file, and production can move forward very efficiently. Treating a CSS somewhat like we do a DTD, we find that in the real world we are better off recycling a document of that type (one of write once, read many) rather than creating a new one for every XML document. By constantly evolving and refining style sheets and using styles thoughtfully, XML can become as easy as HTML or XHTML when being presented to a standard browser.

Review Questions

4.1 What are the three basic types of style that create the cascade in CSS?

4.2 What is their order of precedence?

4.3 What are two components of a declaration?

4.4 Name three subcomponents and provide a brief description of the components that make up XSL.

4.5 Which of these is *not* one of the eight border styles?

```
dotted
dashed
solid
single
double
groove
ridge
inset
outset
```

4.6 What is the default value for background?
  a. white
  b. transparent
  c. inherited
  d. black

4.7 Which one of these PI examples is correct?
  a. `<!-- xml-stylesheet type="text/css" href="my_css.css" -->`
  b. `<?xml-stylesheet type="text/css" href="my_CSS.css"?>`
  c. `<? xml-stylesheet style="text/css" href="my_CSS.css" ?>`
  d. `<? xml-stylesheet style="text/css" href="my_CSS.css" />`

4.8 What was added for use with *fonts* to the CSS specification in CSS2?

4.9 Give an example of one of the answers from Question 4.8, and explain its use and syntax.

4.10 What are three properties of the *border* style?

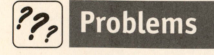

Problems

Use this example XML document to create a style sheet (CSS) to present it in a Web browser.

```
<cd>
<title>Beautiful Maladies</title>
<artist>
<firstname>Tom</firstname>
<lastname>Waits</lastname>
</artist>
<song genre="urban folk" year="1987" length="2:42"> Hang on St.
      Christopher</song>
<song genre="urban folk" year="1987" length="3:51">
      Temptation</song>
<song genre="urban folk" year="1985" length="3:45"> Clap
      Hands</song>
</cd>
```

Use the DTD created in Chapter 2:

```
<!DOCTYPE title [
<!ELEMENT CD (title, artist+, song*)>
<!ELEMENT title (#PCDATA)>
<!ELEMENT artist ((firstname*, lastname) | group?)>
<!ELEMENT firstname (#PCDATA)>
<!ELEMENT lastname (#PCDATA)>
<!ELEMENT group (#PCDATA)>
<!ELEMENT song (#PCDATA)>
<!ATTLIST song genre CDATA #IMPLIED>
<!ATTLIST song year CDATA #IMPLIED>
<!ATTLIST song length CDATA #IMPLIED>
]>
```

4.1 Declare a font color of red and weight of 400 for the `title` element.

4.2 Declare a font size and weight for the `song` element.

4.3 Add the `notes` element and declare the `display: block` style in the DTD.

4.4 Create a text shadow for the `artist` element.

4.5 Place all these in a style sheet named `cd.css`, and link it in the XML document by creating the appropriate PI.

Answers to Review Questions

4.1 Author, user, user agent (UA).

4.2 UA overrides user, which overrides author.

4.3 Property and value.

4.4 XPath, which is a language for referencing specific parts of an XML document; XSLT, which is a language for describing how to transform one XML document (represented as a tree) into another; and XSL, which is XSLT plus a description of a set of formatting objects and formatting properties.

4.5 `solid`; all the others are border styles.

4.6 b. `transparent`.

4.7 b. All the others have syntax errors.

4.8 `text-shadow`, `font-size-adjust`, and `font-stretch`.

4.9 `h3 { text-shadow: 3px 4px 5px red }`.

4.10 `width`, `border-style`, `color`.

Solutions to Problems

4.1 `title { font-color: red; font-weight: 400}` or `title { font-color: 255-0-0; font-weight: 400}`.

4.2 `song { font-size: 14px; font-weight: 400}`.

4.3 Modify the root declaration:

```
<!ELEMENT CD (title, artist+, song*, notes?)>
```

Add this element:

```
<!ELEMENT notes (#PCDATA)>
```

Declare the style:

```
notes { display: inline; font-weight: bold }
```

4.4 `artist { text-shadow: 3px 4px 5px red }`.

4.5 Save in a text editor as `cd.css`:

```
title { font-color: red; font-weight: 400}
song { font-size: 14px; font-weight: 400}
notes { display: inline; font-weight: bold }
artist { text-shadow: 3px 4px 5px red }
```

Use this PI:

```
<?xml-stylesheet type="text/css" href="cd.css"?>
```

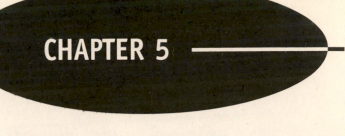

CHAPTER 5

DOM and SAX

5.1   Levels of DOM

The Document Object Model (DOM) provides a standard set of *objects* and *methods* for representing Hypertext Markup Language (HTML) and Extensible Markup Language (XML) documents. It creates a standard model of how these objects can be combined as well as a standard interface to access and manipulate them. The DOM, as it is commonly known, serves as an application programming interface (API) that allows vendors or authors to write to or support this API instead of creating their own proprietary or product-specific APIs, therefore increasing interoperability of the Web. In essence, the DOM defines an important model that programmers can use to help their code interact with XML documents.

The levels and specifications of the DOM are governed by the World Wide Web Consortium (W3C) and therefore represent the standard for accessing content in XML documents. The DOM represents an XML document as a tree of *nodes* that map their order and structure to the document's elements. Each node in the tree may be accessed randomly and readily. As the middle term of the model (object) indicates, the DOM takes documents, arranges their elements to be accessible as objects, following the organization of the document's internal structure. This approach makes the DOM easy to navigate and follow; also, its object orientation makes it familiar to Java programmers or those who use other object-oriented languages.

To quote from a W3C Activity Statement:

> W3C's Document Object Model (DOM) is a standard API (application
> programming interface) to the document structure and aims to make it easy
> for programmers to access components and delete, add or edit their content,
> attributes and style. In essence, the DOM makes it possible for programmers
> to write applications which will work properly on all browsers and servers,
> and on all platforms. While programmers may need to use different
> programming languages, they do not need to change their programming
> model.

The W3C describes the DOM as a "platform- and language-neutral interface that will allow programs and scripts to dynamically access and update the content, structure and style of documents. The document can be further processed, and the results of that processing can be incorporated back into the presented page." (See "Add") www.w3.org/DOM/.

The levels of the DOM are still evolving, where each new level builds on preceding levels with increased complexity and versatility. The initial DOM described only a few methods, such as a method to access an identifier by name or through a particular link. Functionality equivalent to that included in Netscape Navigator 3.0 and Microsoft Internet Explorer 3.0 is referred to as *DOM level 0*.

Level 1, on the other hand, focuses on the core document model, primarily HTML, and provides methods for document navigation and manipulation. The level 1 DOM is considered the *core* object model by virtue of its basic functionality. An object model is created in the memory of the user agent, and defines the core tree (node) structure that subsequent levels build on.

Level 2 adds a style sheet object model and defines functionality to manipulate style information attached to a document. It also enables traversal of the document, defines an event model, and provides support for XML namespaces.

Level 3 addresses document loading and saving, as well as content models, such as Document Type Definitions (DTDs) and schemas, with document validation support. In addition, level 3 also addresses document views and formatting, key events, and event groups.

Level 4 and beyond should ". . . specify some interface with a possible underlying window system, including some ways to prompt the user. They may also contain a query language interface and address multithreading and synchronization, security, and repository."

At this point, level 3 is at the Working Draft stage, and level 4 and beyond are just speculation. Level 2 became a Recommendation in November of 2000. As a W3C specification, the guiding objective for the XML DOM is to provide a standard programming interface to XML documents for a wide variety of applications. The XML DOM is designed to be used with any programming language and any operating system.

5.2　XML Tree Structure

With the XML DOM, a programmer can create an XML document, navigate its structure, and add, modify, or delete its elements. The key to understanding and using the DOM is to grasp the underlying tree structure that is built in the client memory and allows access to the API. The API is the *interface* to the document and allows the document to be manipulated during parsing.

The documentElement is the top level of the tree. The documentElement may contain many branches, which are referred to as *nodes*. The *node interface* is the primary datatype for the entire DOM. It represents a single node in the document tree. It may contain a childNode, depending on its definition (not all allow descendants). Examples of nodes that do not allow children are

`DocumentType`, `ProcessingInstruction`, `Comment`, `Text`, and `CDATASection`. Each of these `childNodes` represents another tree branch and can be accessed individually via properties and methods. Nodes may be referenced as *ancestors,* which is any node *X above* (toward the root) from the node *Y*. A descendant node is any node *Z* that is *below* the node *Y*. A *parent* node is the immediate ancestor node. In addition, two nodes are considered equivalent if they have the same node type and name. Figure 5-1 shows the basic tree structure of an XML DOM.

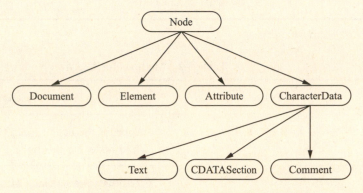

Fig. 5-1.   The basic tree structure of an XML DOM.

A node property will return a value (or list of values) for the node. For instance, the `childNodes` property returns a `NodeList` containing all the child nodes for that node. Another property is `nodeValue`, which returns, or sets, the value of this node, depending on the type. A `method` allows the node to be manipulated by an operation or function. Table 5-1 shows a list of typical node properties from `www.w3schools.com`. Table 5-2 presents a generalized list of methods from `www.w3schools.com`.

Table 5-1 Typical Node Properties

Name	Description
`attributes`	Returns a `NamedNodeMap` containing all attributes for this node.
`childNodes`	Returns a `NodeList` containing all the child nodes for this node.
`firstChild`	Returns the first child node for this node.
`lastChild`	Returns the last child node for this node.
`nextSibling`	Returns the next sibling node. Two nodes are siblings if they have the same parent node.
`nodeName`	Returns the `nodeName`, depending on the type.

nodeType	Returns the nodeType as a number.
nodeValue	Returns, or sets, the value of this node, depending on the type.
ownerDocument	Returns the root node of the document.
parentNode	Returns the parent node for this node.
previousSibling	Returns the previous sibling node. Two nodes are siblings if they have the same parent node.

Table 5-2   Methods for Use with Nodes

Name	Description
appendChild(newChild)	Appends the node newChild at the end of the child nodes for this node.
cloneNode(boolean)	Returns an exact clone of this node. If the boolean value is set to true, the cloned node contains all the child nodes as well.
hasChildNodes()	Returns true if this node has any child nodes.
insertBefore(newNode,refNode)	Inserts a new node newNode before the existing node refNode.
removeChild(nodeName)	Removes the specified node nodeName.
replaceChild(newNode,oldNode)	Replaces oldNode with the newNode.

In summary:

- Child element A is called the child of element B if and only if element B is the parent of element A.
- Descendant element A is called a descendant of element B if either element A is a child of element B or element A is the child of element C that is a descendant of element B.
- Ancestor element A is called an ancestor of element B if and only if element B is a descendant of element A.
- Sibling element A is called a sibling of element B if and only if elements B and A share the same parent element. Element A is a preceding sibling if it comes before element B in the document tree. Element A is a following sibling if it comes after element B in the document tree.

5.3   The DOM Core

Level 1 of the XML DOM is considered the core of the API. It provides a basic but essential collection of objects and interfaces useful to access and manipulate document objects. Again, the W3C says it best:

> The DOM Level 1 specification is separated into two parts: Core and HTML. The Core DOM Level 1 section provides a low-level set of fundamental interfaces that can represent any structured document, as well as defining extended interfaces for representing an XML document. These extended XML interfaces need not be implemented by a DOM implementation that only provides access to HTML documents; all of the fundamental interfaces in the Core section must be implemented. A compliant DOM implementation that implements the extended XML interfaces is required to also implement the fundamental Core interfaces, but not the HTML interfaces. The HTML Level 1 section provides additional, higher-level interfaces that are used with the fundamental interfaces defined in the Core Level 1 section to provide a more convenient view of an HTML document. A compliant implementation of the HTML DOM implements all of the fundamental Core interfaces as well as the HTML interfaces.

Remember that the Document Object Model represents an XML document as a tree or hierarchy of node objects, where other more specialized interfaces are also available. The node interface is the primary datatype for the entire DOM. It represents a single node in the document tree. Although all objects implementing the node interface expose methods for dealing with children, not all objects implementing the node interface may have children. Some types of nodes may have child nodes of various types, and others may be leaf nodes that cannot have anything below them in the document structure.

The node types and the node types that they may have as children are as follows:

- *Document*. Element (maximum of one), `ProcessingInstruction`, `Comment`, and `DocumentType`.
- *DocumentFragment*. Element, `ProcessingInstruction`, `Comment`, `Text`, `CDATASection`, and `EntityReference`.
- *EntityReference*. Element, `ProcessingInstruction`, `Comment`, `Text`, `CDATASection`, and `EntityReference`.
- *Element*. Element, `Text`, `Comment`, `ProcessingInstruction`, `CDATASection`, and `EntityReference`.
- *Attr*. `Text` and `EntityReference`.
- *Entity*. Element, `ProcessingInstruction`, `Comment`, `Text`, `CDATASection`, and `EntityReference`.

`DocumentType`, `ProcessingInstruction`, `Comment`, `Text`, `CDATASection`, and `Notation` may not have any children.

5.4 Using DOM Interfaces

Beyond manual editing and translation of XML documents, it will be useful for the user to be able to manipulate XML content using DOM calls. This is where the DOM interface comes into play. By accessing properties of the DOM through the various methods, you can create a platform-independent and language-neutral interface. This interface is a precursor to more complex APIs such as SAX. Most of these properties and methods are built into DOM level 0 or 1 and, as a result, are widely available for most applications.

The *object* in the Document Object Model may be a bit misleading, much like the *Java* in JavaScript. The properties of the DOM are not accessed as objects in the truest sense but rather through the interface.

Using a simple example, we can inspect the DOM interface. In this case we will use

```
<parent><child name="child1">text to
        display</child></parent>
```

This looks simple enough, but how is it represented in the DOM? Figure 5-2 shows how the previous markup is represented in the DOM.

So how do we access these individual nodes? Through the DOM interface and its properties and methods. For example, if you want to extract the contents of the element

```
<child name="child1">text to display</child>
```

you can access the contents using the `getNodeValue()` method. You accomplish this by a series of steps, accessing the properties and values along the way. The actual code depends on the XML parser being used, such as Sun TreeWalker or MSXML.

First, you bring in the document via the DOM interface using `Node`. The node is the heart of the DOM interface and is a logical and likely starting point. The node interface defines a number of methods, and the ones you will use are `getNodeName()`, which returns the name of the node, `getNodeValue()`, which returns the value of the node, `hasChildNodes()`, which returns a Boolean true or false, `getFirstChild()`, and `getNextSibling()`.

If there are children, that is, `hasChildNodes()=true`, you can use them as stepping-stones or waypoints to navigate the node structure of the document. From here, you can call `getFirstChild()` and `getNextSibling()`. Using only these two methods, you can traverse the entire tree. The other methods (`getLastChild()`, `getPreviousSibling()`, `getParentNode()`, etc.) provide convenience when returning to the top of the tree and are very handy on a document of any size, but for a small example like this, these two will do just fine for navigation.

Thus you start at the `<parent>` node, test for children (`true`), and `getFirstChild()`. At this point you can call `getNodeName()`, and if it is the one you want, you can call `getNodeValue()`. If the name of the node is not the one you want, you can call `getNextSibling()`.

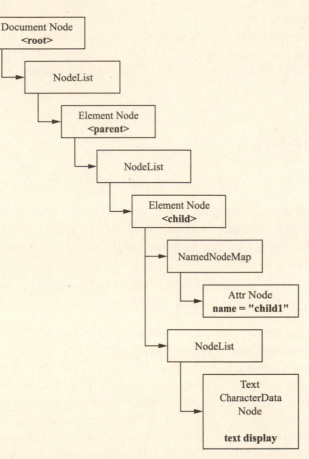

Fig. 5-2.   The markup `<parent><child name="child1">text to display</child></parent>` as represented in the DOM.

5.5   DOM Views

A document may have one or more views associated with it; that is, there may be a computed view on a document *after* applying a Cascading Style Sheet (CSS) or multiple presentations of the same document in a client. A view is some alternate representation or presentation of a source document.

A view may be *static,* reflecting the state of the document when the view was created, or *dynamic,* reflecting changes in the target document just before the view was created.

The level 2 DOM views are rather limited, but level 3 seems to be shaping up as quite a bit more robust. Some of the proposed features include *segments,* which are distinct portions of a view, and *view,* which is a new interface that is the *root* for segments. Also added is `Match` (and its relatives `MatchString`, `MatchInteger`, `MatchBoolean`, etc.), which allows a portion of a segment to be compared with a stated value and an item returned if it exists. All these interfaces have an Interface Definition Language (IDL) definition for use in the API and are used in the fashion of DOM-style interfaces.

In practice, views can be applied based on agent needs and can respond to events that are accessible through the DOM interface. For a full treatment of level 3 views, see the Working Drafts (`www.w3.org/TR/2001/WD-DOM-Level-3-XPath-20010618/`) and eventual Recommendation at W3C's Web site.

5.6　DOM Events

The DOM level 2 event model is designed with two primary goals:

- To create an *event system* that allows the use of event handlers, such as mouse events and the like, to register within the DOM. This will allow event-driven flow through the tree structure and provide a standard framework for user interface and control.

- To maintain a compatibility with level 0 scripts and content to not render obsolete the earlier system by the level 0 browsers.

The event model should be familiar to anyone who has used JavaScript, Visual Basic, or another event-driven programming language. For review, when an event occurs on a document, such as when a user clicks on a link, a special object, called an *event object,* is created. Basically, an event object is a specialized container for information about activities related to some specific document object. It keeps track of the type of event that occurs (onmousedown, onmouseup, mouseover, click, double-click, etc.) and may even record key sequences at the time an event occurs (for additional processing). When an event occurs, it does not remain in the same spot where it occurred. Rather, it travels (or flows) through the document and the elements in the page until it can travel no more. Because events can occur at any time, and are usually associated with one or more document objects, programmers create special methods called *event handlers* to detect and respond to event objects as they're encountered.

The Netscape Navigator team created the concept of an event capture, in that Navigator recognizes and catches events as they attach themselves to some target element. Thus, clicking on a link starts an event at the document level (at the root of the node tree) and travels toward the specific link object itself. Navigators' `captureEvents` method lets programmers intercept the event before it reaches the target link, so a handler can intervene, perform one or more tasks (change the link color, activate another window, or whatever) before the event reaches the target link itself. Unfortunately, this approach prevents the event from returning to the parent element that contains the target, which may cause event information to be discarded or lost.

By contrast, Internet Explorer (IE) reverses this order in a concept known as *event bubbling*. Rather than moving from the document level down to the target element, in IE event information moves up the node tree from the target element to its parent element. The name comes from the ability to intercept events as they "bubble up" from the target element to the visible surface in the browser Window. A possible shortcoming of this approach is that multiple event handlers can only be invoked as they're encountered; though it may be desirable for a higher-level handler to process event data first, sometimes this may not reflect that actual handling order. This explains why most current browsers use a hybrid method, and combine both concepts in their event-handling methods.

The W3C has defined the following terminology for use with DOM events:

- *User-interface (UI) events*. Events that occur because of user interaction with an external device, such as a keyboard or mouse.
- *UI logical events*. UI events, such as element-triggering or focus-change messages.
- *Mutation events*. Events that occur as a result of an action that changes the structure of a document.
- *Capturing*. When an event is handled by an event target's ancestor before it is given to the event's target.
- *Bubbling*. When an event moves upward from the target element to its parent (through its ancestors).
- *Cancelable*. When the client chooses not to allow the DOM implementation to process default actions of an event.

An event flows from the DOM implementation to the DOM. A DOM application may use the `hasFeature(feature, version)` method of the `DOMImplementation` to determine whether the event module is supported by the implementation. Along the way, events will be registered to the DOM, and depending on the event target, the document will respond accordingly.

5.7   DOM Style Interfaces

A primary design goal of the DOM level 2 CSS interface is to allow access to the object model constructs of the document using the familiar property/ method tools. DOM level 2 style sheet interfaces are base interfaces representing a single style sheet associated with a structured document. In HTML, the style sheet interface represents either an external style sheet or an in-line `style` element.

In XML, this interface represents an external style sheet, included through a style sheet processing instruction (PI):

```
<?xml:stylesheet href="example.css" type="text/css"?>
```

A DOM application may use the `hasFeature(feature, version)` method of the `DOMImplementation` interface with parameter values `StyleSheets` and `2.0` in this case to determine whether this module is supported by the implementation. Additionally, an implementation also must support the core feature as defined in the DOM level 2 core specification.

The key to using the DOM level 2 style interface is this structure, known as an *Interface Definition Language (IDL) definition*:

```
IDL Definition
// Introduced in DOM Level 2:
interface StyleSheet {
    readonly attribute DOMString    type;
        attribute boolean    disabled;
    readonly attribute Node       ownerNode;
    readonly attribute StyleSheet    parentStyleSheet;
    readonly attribute DOMString    href;
    readonly attribute DOMString    title;
    readonly attribute MediaList    media;
};
```

Many (if not most) current programming languages, such as Java, C++, and the like, use a variant of the IDL. An *IDL* allows types other than interfaces to be expressed by providing a standardized mechanism for representing data. For example, primitive types such as Boolean, several signed and unsigned integer types, and some floating-point types may be defined.

In our DOM level 2 IDL, we are able to describe the interface StyleSheet. This interface represents the generic notion of IDL. In the DOM level 2, there are three attributes: StyleSheet, StyleSheetList, and MediaList.

We will look at each attribute separately, using the generic IDL, one line at a time. This line is a comment:

```
// Introduced in DOM Level 2:
```

The order of terms is as follows: whether an attribute is read-only, the declaration (attribute), the type, and the name. In the second line of each example, this is rewritten as a sentence.

```
readonly attribute DOMString NameOfAttribute;
```
NameOfAttribute of type *DOMString* (which is) readonly (or not).

This gets easier after you look at a few of them. This basic structural syntax holds throughout DOM IDL use.

```
readonly attribute DOMString type;
```
type of type *DOMString,* readonly

This specifies the style sheet language for this style sheet, specified as a content type, for instance, text/css. This is a readonly attribute.

```
attribute boolean disabled;
```
disabled of type *boolean*

This resolves to false if the style sheet is applied to the document and true if it is not. Modifying this attribute may cause a new resolution of style for the document. A style sheet applies only if both an appropriate medium definition is present and the disabled attribute is false. If the medium does not apply to the current user agent, the disabled attribute is ignored, as it is redundant.

```
readonly attribute Node    ownerNode;
```

ownerNode of type *Node,* readonly

This node associates this style sheet with the document. For HTML, this may be the corresponding link or style element. For XML, it may be the linking PI. For style sheets that are included by other style sheets, the value of this attribute is null.

```
readonly attribute StyleSheet    parentStyleSheet;
```
parentStyleSheet of type *StyleSheet,* readonly

   For style sheet languages that support the concept of style sheet inclusion, this attribute represents the included style sheet, if one exists. If the style sheet is a top-level style sheet, or the style sheet language does not support inclusion, the value of this attribute is null. This is a readonly attribute.

```
readonly attribute DOMString href;
```
href of type *DOMString,* readonly

If the style sheet is a linked style sheet, the value of its attribute is its location. For in-line style sheets, the value of this attribute is null. Again, it is readonly.

```
readonly attribute DOMString title;
```
title of type *DOMString,* readonly

The advisory is title. The title is often specified in the ownerNode. Again, it is readonly.

```
readonly attribute MediaList media;
```
media of type *MediaList,* readonly

This declares the intended destination medium for style information. The medium often is specified in the ownerNode. If no medium has been specified, the MediaList will be empty. Note that modifying the MediaList may cause a change to the attribute disabled. This, too, is readonly.

   The next one is Interface StyleSheetList, also introduced in DOM level 2. The StyleSheetList interface provides the abstraction of an ordered collection of style sheets. The items in the StyleSheetList are accessible via an integral index, starting from 0.

```
IDL Definition
// Introduced in DOM Level 2:
interface StyleSheetList {
    readonly attribute unsigned long length;
    StyleSheet    item(in unsigned long index);
};
```

ATTRIBUTES

```
readonly attribute unsigned long length;
```
    length of type *unsigned long,* readonly

This states the number of StyleSheets in the list. It uses an unsigned long integer as its datatype. The valid range of child style sheet indices is 0 to length-1 (inclusive), with 0 being the first.

METHODS

item

This is used to retrieve a style sheet by its ordinal index. If index is greater than or equal to the number of style sheets in the list, this returns null.

PARAMETERS

index of type *unsigned long*
Index into the collection

This returns the style sheet at the index position in the StyleSheetList or null if this is not a valid index. For instance, to access the third style sheet, request index 2 (since the first is 0).

Interface MediaList (introduced in DOM Level 2)

The MediaList interface provides the abstraction of an ordered collection of media without defining how this collection is actually implemented. An empty list is the same as a list that contains the medium all.

The items in the MediaList are accessible via an integral index, starting from 0, just like the previous interface.

```
IDL Definition
// Introduced in DOM Level 2:
interface MediaList {
    attribute DOMString mediaText;
// raises(DOMException) on setting
    readonly attribute unsigned long length;
    DOMString item (in unsigned long index);
    void deleteMedium(in DOMString oldMedium)
        raises(DOMException);
    void appendMedium(in DOMString newMedium)
        raises(DOMException);
};
```

Here, we dissect this IDL one line at a time:

```
IDL Definition
// Introduced in DOM Level 2:
interface MediaList {
```

This first part is the beginning of the IDL declaration and a comment. Next, we have

```
attribute DOMString mediaText;
```
mediaText of type *DOMString*

This is a comma-separated list of media, a parsable textual representation of the media list. Following this, we have another comment. Then:

```
readonly attribute unsigned long length;
```
length of type *unsigned long,* readonly

This is an unsigned long integer stating the number of media in the list. The range of valid media is 0 to length-1 (inclusive), same as the others. This attribute is readonly.

Very similar to length is item, which looks like the next line:

```
DOMString item (in unsigned long index);
```
item of type *DOMString*

This allows us to access the next item in the index. If item is greater than (or equal to) the number of media in MediaList, then this will return null. Now we get into something a bit different. The next lines are of the type void, which specifies the type of an operation that does not return a value. Also, these can raise an exception.

```
void deleteMedium (in DOMString oldMedium)
        raises(DOMException);
void appendMedium (in DOMString newMedium)
        raises(DOMException);
void deleteMedium(in DOMString oldMedium)
        raises(DOMException);
void appendMedium(in DOMString newMedium)
        raises(DOMException);
```

Both of these, deleteMedium and appendMedium, are of type void found in DOMString oldMedium or newMedium. The only method for this IDL is appendMedium, which adds the medium (newMedium) to the end of the list. If the newMedium is already used, it is removed first.

These are the exceptions on setting MediaList (which are raised if there is an error):

- SYNTAX_ERR. Raised if the specified string value has a syntax error and is unparsable.

- NO_MODIFICATION_ALLOWED_ERR. Raised if this media list is read-only.

5.8   DOM Traversal and Ranges

The navigation, or stepping from node to node within the XML document by the parser, is known as *traversing*. The DOM provides tools in the API for ordered movement between nodes and their ancestors, children, and siblings. A *range* indicates the content contained between two specified end points as one contiguous selection. A range interface confers the advantage of being able to access and manipulate entire portions of a document tree at a higher-level, rather than requiring that the range be decomposed into a sequence of nodes, each of which must be handled separately. See the W3C DOM core for full details.

A *range* is comprised of two *boundary points* representing the start and end of the range. The positions of the boundary points in a document (or `DocumentFragment`) tree consist of a starting node address and an offset (or range of nodes within the DOM's internal tree structure). The starting node address becomes the container for the boundary point and its position in the tree. This container and its ancestors are also ancestors to the boundary point and its position in the tree as well, so they may be used for navigation purposes. Likewise, the offset within node becomes the offset of the boundary point and its position in the tree. If the container node is of type `Attr`, `Document`, `DocumentFragment`, `Element`, or `EntityReference`, that offset occurs before its child nodes; but if the container node is of type `CharacterData`, `Comment`, or `ProcessingInstruction` (PI), the offset occurs before the string value for the node.

The boundary points of a range must share a common ancestor, which is either a `Document`, `DocumentFragment`, or `Attr` node. That is, the content of a range must be entirely within the subtree rooted by a single `Document`, `DocumentFragment`, or `Attr` node. This common ancestor container is known as the *root container* of the range. The tree rooted by the root container is known as the range's *context tree*.

When navigating XML documents, the traversal-range recommendation defines two separate interfaces for XML elements. The `NodeIterator` interface provides methods to move linearly through a document, traversing it from node to node in the order in which they occur. The `TreeWalker` interface permits traversal of the document as a tree-based structure. To use either of these interfaces, call the `create` method, and set appropriate flags for elements that should be included in the view.

In practice, we would use an application such as Xerces (available from the Apache Software Foundation), which is a Java application that has all the files you need and plenty of documentation. Others are available, of course, from Microsoft, Sun, and other vendors.

To traverse a flat representation of XML, use the `NodeIterator` interface. For example, look at this XML document paraphrased from the site: `http://www.onjava.com/pub/a/onjava/2001/02/08/dom.html?page=2`.

```
<a>
    <b>first text</b>
    <c>
        <d>a child of c</d>
        <e>another child of c, sibling to d</e>
    </c>
    <f>some more text</f>
```

```
    <g>still more text</g>
</a>
```

When this is flattened, it gives us the nodes: a b c d e f g. When we traverse these nodes, we get what is called a *horizontal version* of the XML document.

The other approach is to use the `TreeWalker` interface, which allows us to approach the tree structure of the XML document using the parent and child nodes. The `TreeWalker` interface provides the methods for jumping from node to node via `parentNode()`, `firstChild()`, `lastChild()`, `previousSibling()`, `nextSibling()`, and so on, as well as the more linear `previousNode()` and `nextNode()`. As we saw in the section on using DOM interfaces, the entire XML document can be traversed using just `firstChild()` and `nextSibling()`. However, as a matter of practicality, we most likely would take advantage of the convenience offered by the full list of methods.

Using the `TreeWalker` interface, the entire XML document is parsed by traversing each branch of the tree in turn using `nextNode()` as the primary method. The output from this method is often identical to the `NodeIterator` interface with the hierarchy of the original tree retained, even though some nodes may be missing, and therefore has methods to move up and down in the tree as well as back and forth.

To allow for simplified document editing, use the range module, which is a set of high-level methods. A range is created by calling the `createRange()` method on the `DocumentRange` interface. This interface can be obtained from the object implementing the document interface using binding-specific casting methods.

```
interface DocumentRange {
    Range createRange();
}
```

The default or initial state of the range returned by the `createRange()` method is that both its boundary points are positioned at the beginning of the corresponding document, before any content. In other words, the container of each boundary point is the document node, and the offset within that node is 0. The range is defined by the boundary points of a range, which occur within a container at a specified offset.

A range's position, other than the default, can be specified by setting the container and the offset of each boundary point with the `setStart()` and `setEnd()` methods:

```
void setStart(in Node parent, in long offset)
        raises(RangeException);
void setEnd(in Node parent, in long offset)
        raises(RangeException);
```

Using these methods, each instance of `createRange()` is unique to the document that is calling it. In addition, keep in mind that the *start* position of a range can never be after the end position.

5.9   The Sax Interface

SAX, the *Simple API for XML*, is a standard interface for event-based XML parsing, whereas the DOM interface is tree-based. (It produces a tree of `xmlNode` structures that the parser traverses.)

SAX is most effective for processing a small subset of a large XML document. SAX allows you to efficiently locate a specific part(s) of the document without the processing time required for creating a tree view, as required in the DOM interface.

SAX is event-based, so when the SAX parser comes to a specified element in the XML document, it treats it like an event, and calls the appropriate code for that event. The SAX parser uses callback methods to let you know a specific item has been found in the document. Some of the more common callbacks are `startDocument`, `endDocument`, `startElement`, `endElement`, `getEntity`, and `characters`. Most of these are fairly self-explanatory. The `characters` callback is called when characters *outside* a tag are parsed.

Before we look at the SAX interface closely, we should be aware of a few simple things. First, as of this writing, SAX 2.0.1 is the current implementation. In addition, SAX is not a full XML parser but rather a set of Java interfaces and helper classes that must be implemented by any parser that wants to be compliant with SAX 2.0.1. (SAX is mainly used with XML and Java, although it can also be used with Python, Perl, or C++.)

The SAX 2.0.1 interfaces, classes, and exceptions are

Package org.xml.sax
Interfaces

- `Attributes`
- `ContentHandler`
- `DTDHandler`
- `EntityResolver`
- `ErrorHandler`
- `Locator`
- `XMLFilter`
- `XMLReader`

Classes

- `InputSource`

Exceptions

- `SAXException`
- `SAXNotRecognizedException`
- `SAXNotSupportedException`
- `SAXParseException`

Package org.xml.sax.helpers
Classes

- `AttributesImpl`
- `DefaultHandler`
- `LocatorImpl`
- `NamespaceSupport`
- `ParserAdapter`
- `XMLFilterImpl`
- `XMLReaderAdapter`
- `XMLReaderFactory`

The most important and immediately useful of these are the different handler interfaces (that is, `ContentHandler`, `DTDHandler`, etc.).

The `ContentHandler` interface, for example, specifies all the callback methods that will be used to deliver information about

- The *document* starting and ending elements
- An XML element's starting and ending points
- Namespaces and attributes for elements
- Namespace prefix mapping
- Processing instructions
- White space and character data

There are four main handlers in SAX:

- `EntityResolver`
- `DTDHandler`
- `DocumentHandler`
- `ErrorHandler`

Looking closer at `DocumentHandler`, we see that it contains the following methods:

- Public abstract void `startDocument()` throws a `SAXException` error.
- Public abstract void `endDocument()` throws a `SAXException` error.
- Public abstract void `startElement(String name, AttributeList atts)` throws a `SAXException` error.
- Public abstract void `endElement(String name)` throws a `SAXException` error.

These are a bit reminiscent of the IDL interface in syntax by declaring scope (public), datatype, and the like. When working with handlers, you need to *implement* the abstract functions of the handler, *instantiate* a new handler, and *set* the handler to the parser.

To use SAX to read XML, you create an instance of a parser object that is pointed to your document and to your application. While SAX reads the document, it calls the `startElement` (the start tag), `endElement` (the end tag), and `characters` (text data in between) as it goes.

The SAX parser reads the XML file (also a DTD if it is present), and when it encounters something such as an element, it generates an event. On recognition of such an event, your program can register with the parser as a listener by implementing certain interfaces. The SAX parser then calls certain methods, which you have overridden to do what you need to do in response to the event. Although the SAX parser organizes its events a bit differently, the situation is similar to an Abstract Window Toolkit (AWT) button generating `ActionEvents` when clicked. Then an interested class implements an `ActionListener` and overrides the callback method `actionPerformed`.

SAX events, unlike AWT events, come in an ordered sequence as the XML file is read in. Given the tree structure of the XML file, the parser generates events in a *depth-first* order. Furthermore, because the events are triggered on the fly as the XML file is read in, you only get one chance to grab an event as it goes by. You must do something to capture relevant information at the point at which it arrives, or the information is lost unless you parse the entire file again. This is in contrast to the DOM parser, which reads the entire document in, storing it in its tree structure in memory, and then waits for your program to analyze it.

The steps are

1. Obtain a SAX parser for your system (such as Xerces from Apache).
2. Provide a document handler (usually a Java class).
3. Customize error handling for the software used (also Java-based).
4. Use a validating parser for the XML (Xerces again).

To understand how an event-based API works, consider the following sample document:

```
<?xml version="1.0"?>
<doc>
<greeting>Hi everyone!</greeting>
</doc>
```

An event-based interface will break the structure of this document into a series of linear events:

```
start document
start element: doc
start element: greeting
characters: Hello everyone!
end element: greeting
end element: doc
end document
```

Here is an example of a simple SAX routine (aka Java):

```
import org.xml.sax.HandlerBase;
import org.xml.sax.AttributeList;
public class MyHandler extends HandlerBase
{
public void startElement (String name, AttributeList atts)
{
System.out.println("Start element: " + name);
}
public void endElement (String name)
{
System.out.println("End element: " + name);
}
}
```

Review Questions

5.1 What does the DOM use for accessing and manipulating objects in the document?
   a. Properties and methods
   b. Attributes and elements
   c. Comments
   d. Processing instructions

5.2 Is the DOM specific to any particular platform or operating system?

5.3 Which level of the DOM is considered the core?

5.4 The DOM is considered to be what type of structure?
   a. Branching
   b. Linear
   c. Tree
   d. Text

5.5 Which of the following cannot contain children?
   a. DocumentType
   b. ProcessingInstruction
   c. Comment
   d. Text
   e. CDATASection
   f. Notation
   g. All of the above
   h. None of the above

5.6 What is the node B directly above node A called?
   a. Father
   b. Mother

    c. Ancestor

    d. Child

5.7 What are nodes that share a common ancestor called?

    a. Cousins

    b. Siblings

    c. Related

    d. Friends

5.8 In the DOM level 2 event model, what is meant by a UI event?

5.9 What is meant by a mutation event?

5.10 What was added in DOM level 2?

    a. Handling namespaces

    b. Handling document events

    c. Traversing the document

    d. Exposing generic and CSS style scripts in the document

    e. Representing views of the document

    f. All of the above

5.11 Which of these are DOM level 2 interfaces?

    a. `StyleSheet`

    b. `StyleSheetList`

    c. `MediaList`

    d. All of the above

5.12 What is the content contained *between* two end points called?

    a. Range

    b. Content

    c. Traverse

    d. All of the above

5.13 What is the SAX interface based on?

    a. Events

    b. Trees

    c. Elements

    d. Nodes

5.14 What is the SAX package made up of?

    a. Interfaces

    b. Classes

    c. Exceptions

    d. All of the above

5.15 What are the two types of traversal methods?

5.16 What are the four main handlers in the SAX interface?

5.17 When using handlers in the IDL definition, we must

    a. implement the abstract functions of the handler.

    b. instantiate a new handler.

    c. set the handler to the parser.

    d. do all of the above.

5.18 When using a TreeWalker interface,

    a. the entire XML document is parsed by traversing each branch of the tree.

    b. some nodes of the XML document are parsed.

    c. siblings are parsed.

    d. parents are walked.

5.19 Is the output from the `TreeWalker` different from that of the `NodeIterator`?

5.20 Is one method (`TreeWalker` versus `NodeIterator`) better than the other?

Problem

Given the DTD and XML document of Chapter 2, namely:

```
<!ELEMENT motionpicture (title, year, genre, director)>

<!ELEMENT title (#PCDATA)>
    <!ATTLIST title language CDATA #IMPLIED>
    <!ATTLIST title alternate_title CDATA #IMPLIED>
    <!ATTLIST title country CDATA #IMPLIED>
    <!ATTLIST title certification #IMPLIED>
    <!ATTLIST title runtime #IMPLIED>

<!ELEMENT year (#PCDATA)>
    <!ATTLIST year academy_awards  CDATA #IMPLIED>
    <!ATTLIST year distributor CDATA #IMPLIED>

<!ELEMENT genre (#PCDATA)>
    <!ATTLIST genre category CDATA #IMPLIED>
    <!ATTLIST genre medium CDATA #IMPLIED>

<!ELEMENT director (#PCDATA)>
    <!ATTLIST director director_of_photography CDATA #IMPLIED>
    <!ATTLIST director cinematographer CDATA #IMPLIED>
    <!ATTLIST director editor CDATA #IMPLIED>
```

5.1 What would the output be as a flat representation?

Answers to Review Questions

5.1 a. Properties and methods

5.2 No, it is a "platform- and language-neutral interface."

5.3 Level 1 is considered the core, and levels 2 and beyond are built on that level.

5.4 c. The DOM is a tree structure.

5.5 g. All of the above cannot have child nodes.

5.6 c. Ancestor

5.7 b. Sibling nodes

5.8 A user-interface event. These events are generated by user interaction through an external device (mouse, keyboard, etc.).

5.9 Events caused by any action that modifies the structure of the document.

5.10 f. All of these were added.

5.11 d. All of them are included in the DOM level 2.

5.12 a. Range is the content contained between two end points.

5.13 a. SAX is a standard interface for event-based XML parsing.

5.14 d. All of the above

5.15 `TreeWalker` and `NodeIterator`

5.16 `EntityResolver`, `DTDHandler`, `DocumentHandler`, and `ErrorHandler`

5.17 d. do all of the above.

5.18 a. the entire XML document is parsed by traversing each branch of the tree.

5.19 No, the output from the `TreeWalker` interface is often identical to the `NodeIterator` interface with the hierarchy of the original tree retained.

5.20 No, they both have their strong points. The `TreeWalker` allows more freedom to move forward and back, and the `NodeIterator` is better suited to large documents.

 # Solution to Problem

5.1 The output as a horizontal representation of the elements would be

```
motionpicture    title    year    genre    director
```

The attributes do not get parsed, only the elements. The entire representation is made up of elements, starting at the top, or root, and migrating from there.

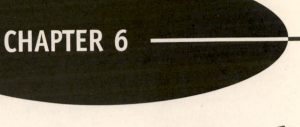

CHAPTER 6

XPath

6.1   Location Paths

The XML Path Language (XPath) is a World Wide Web Consortium (W3C)–defined declarative language used to traverse the Document Object Model (DOM) based on the DOM's tree-node structure. XPath is a mechanism to identify and access portions or subsets of Extensible Markup Language (XML) documents. XPath uses a path-based syntax that is very similar to other traversal syntax used in file systems or document retrieval. XPath is a direct result of the needs of addressing, used in XPointer (see Chapter 8), and pattern matching, used in the Extensible Stylesheet Language Transformations (XSLT, covered in Chapter 7). It provides a common foundation for solving a fundamental problem, which is the need to locate elements, attributes, and other XML document nodes in a concise and convenient way.

According to the W3C, XPath's primary purpose is to address parts of an XML document. It also provides basic facilities for manipulation of strings, numbers, and Booleans. XPath uses a compact, non-XML syntax to facilitate use of XPath within Uniform Resource Identifiers (URIs) and XML attribute values. XPath operates on the abstract, logical structure of an XML document rather than on its surface syntax.

The key, or core, concept to XPath is the *location path*. This allows almost a trickle-down or cascading technique, where each node of the location path is indicated in a directory-like fashion, familiar to anyone with a DOS or UNIX background. The node tree replaces the tree of the directory, but the syntax similarity between them is very consistent. The basic construct of the location path is a sequence of location steps separated by a slash (/). A location path is evaluated compositionally left-to-right, starting with some initial context.

Each node resulting from the evaluation of one step is used as context for evaluation of the next step, and the results are strung together.

The context consists of a context node, a context position, and size (two integers, $1<=position<=size$), variable bindings (a function library and a set of namespace declarations), and the externally defined initial context (for example, by XPointer or Extensible Stylesheet Language Transformations, or XSLT).

For the examples of syntax, we'll start with a document with the node (element) structure that appears in Figure 6-1.

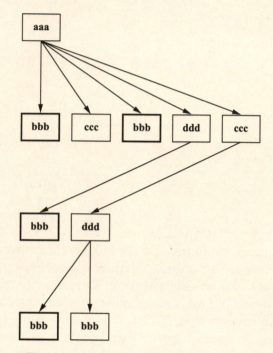

Fig. 6-1.　Node element structure.

This translates to

```
<aaa>
    <bbb/>
    <ccc/>
    <bbb/>
    <ddd>
        <bbb/>
    </ddd>
    <ccc>
        <ddd>
            <bbb/>
            <bbb/>
        </ddd>
    </ccc>
</aaa>
```

The syntax and characters used in XPath are shown in Table 6-1 (again, very similar to file system paths).

Table 6-1 Syntax and Characters
Used in XPath

Character	Description
/	Root node
//	Descendant (or self) node
.	Self node
..	Parent node

If the path starts with a slash (/), it represents an absolute path to the required element. An easy example is /aaa, which selects the root element aaa and looks similar to Figure 6-2.

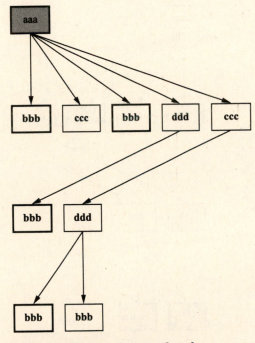

Fig. 6-2. **The root element selected.**

Another simple example is

/aaa/ddd/bbb

which selects all elements bbb that are children of ddd that are children of the root element aaa, as shown in Figure 6-3.

Or another example is //bbb, which selects all bbb elements, as shown in Figure 6-4.

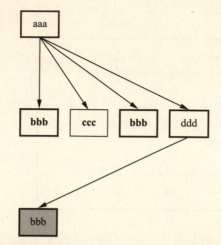

Fig. 6-3.   All bbb elements that are children of ddd selected.

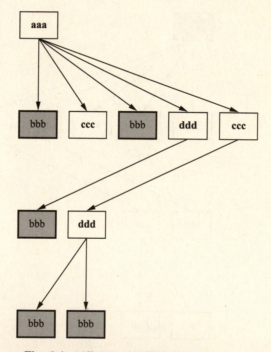

Fig. 6-4.   All bbb elements selected.

Another example is /aaa/ccc, which selects all elements ccc that are children of the root element aaa, as shown in Figure 6-5.

Location path syntax frequently refers to *axes,* which are the relationships between nodes that allow navigation as a reference to the current node, no matter which one it might be. For instance, if a child is referenced, it doesn't matter where it is in the tree; it is the element or node directly descendant from the current node.

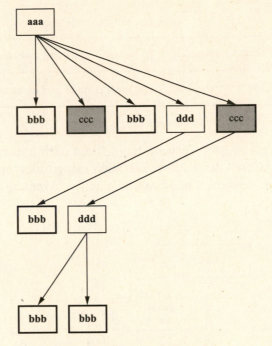

Fig. 6-5. All ccc elements selected.

The axes available in XPath are shown in Table 6-2 (based on the current, or *context*, node).

Table 6-2   Available XPath Axes

Axis	Description
child	Children of the context node
descendant	All descendants
parent	Parent (or direct ancestor)
ancestor	All ancestors between the root and the current parent node
sibling	Nodes with a shared parent
following-sibling	Siblings to the *right* of the context node
preceding-sibling	Siblings to the *left* of the context node
following	*All* following nodes in the document
preceding	*All* preceding nodes in the document

self	The *context* node itself
descendant-or-self	The *context* node and its descendant
ancestor-or-self	The *context* node and its ancestor

Figure 6-6 shows a schematic of these path axis relationships. As you can see, any navigational need can be specified using this syntax. If you look at Figure 6-6, you can see how each node can be reached from any other node using the location path syntax.

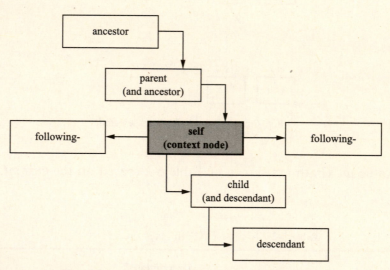

Fig. 6-6.   A schematic of path axis relationships.

6.2   Expressions

Expressions are a key construct of the XPath language. The use of an expression allows you to evaluate a variable or the context of a node. Expressions can consist of a *variable reference,* which evaluates to the value bound to a variable name, or a *function call,* which calls a named function and allows the passing of arguments or testing of the context node as a default and returns a value.

The commonly used expressions are string, number, node set, and Boolean (more about these in detail later in this chapter). The returned value datatype is based on the choice of the function, and an error may be returned if the choice is not appropriate. For example, a string value is returned from a string function and a true or false is returned from a Boolean function. The Boolean is valuable when used with a conditional expression, such as equal to or greater or less than, or a logical expression, such as not, and, or, or a combination of these.

Another type of expression is the *pattern*. Patterns are a limited form of location path used in XSLT (and therefore XML) to describe the step-by-step path needed to reach a desired node from the context node of a given element. The pattern comparison is an implied Boolean, returning true (a match) if the match is found and false (or empty) if it is not.

Using the combination of the attribute `match` and a value for pattern allows a node to be compared for contextual validity and relative location in reference to the current node. A simple example, based on the preceding `/aaa/ccc` location path statement would be indicated as `match="/aaa/ccc"`. This specifies that all `ccc` elements are children of the root element `aaa`. The expression syntax defined in the preceding section also can be used in the match-pattern pair.

Patterns are allowed singularly or in combinations of multiple statements using the proper characters and syntax, such as the | to delineate alternates and so on. Frequently, patterns are used as values in a `select` attribute in XSLT when they cannot be used as a `match` for node sets. This flexibility allows elements to be searched as paths or as a pattern match.

6.3   Core Function Library

Core functions of the XPath language are based on these four basic types:

- Number
- Node set
- Boolean
- String

You should be familiar with these because they are universal to all programming, with some minor exceptions. There is no void type in XPath, and the datatypes are not strongly cast. This provides a bit more flexibility than Java or C++ and is more like JavaScript in its functionality. It is able to convert (within reason) datatypes with the exception of node set arguments, which must be made correctly.

Functions in XPath are indicated by the parenthesis after the function name, as is common practice, and if arguments are to be passed to the function, they are enclosed in the parentheses. For instance, a math function such as `int()` or `round()` will have the value to be acted on passed via the parentheses, that is, `int(1.23)` or `round(4.666)`. The same applies to string functions such as `concat()`, which will concatenate whatever is passed into it. If an argument is optional, it is followed by a question mark (?); otherwise, the argument is required.

Core functions are specified by the W3C and must be included in a function library of any XPath implementation. The full treatment, as always, can be found on the W3C Web site at `www.w3.org/TR/xpath#corelib`.

Node set functions are intended to return a value found at a context reference called by the function. Examples include `last()`, `count()`, `position()`, and `name()`. Most of these are further augmented by indicating the type of value expected, for instance, *number* `last()` or *string* `name()`. Each node set function has a specific intention and should be chosen only if node context is to be interpreted and returned.

This example of the function `id()` will demonstrate how a node set function can be used to access an element either by name or by a combination of name and path. The function `id()` is defined by the W3C as *node-set* `id(object)`.

We can return a `title` element by calling `id()` as

```
id("title")
```

This will return, or select, the element with the unique ID of `title`. Alternatively, we can select an object offset from the specified `title` element using the statement

```
id("title")/child::subtitle[position()=4]
```

which will return the fourth child `subtitle` of the element `title` as a specific element and relative position. The node set functions allow us to access the values of `namespace-uri()` of the document or the context node if left empty (default).

String functions typically are used for operations on strings, such as converting a number to a string (for nonpresentation purposes), or testing the values of a string (or substring) and returning a true or false (Boolean) value. The function `string()` will attempt to convert a number to a string with the following results:

- `NaN` is returned if the value is not a number.
- 0 from positive zero.
- 0 from negative zero.
- `Infinity` from positive infinity.
- `Infinity` from negative infinity.
- Integer form if the value *is* an integer.
- Decimal form if it is not an integer, including the decimal point with at least one digit before and one digit after the decimal point.

The `string()` function will try to convert to one of the four basic types and failing that will convert to a string in a way that is consistent with that type. However, most of the time the result will fall into one of the four basic datatypes.

String functions are typical of most programming or scripting languages with no real surprises. The versatility, or scope, of these functions does not begin to approach that of string functions found in Perl, PHP, or any language that is strong in regular expressions. However, remember that most of the functionality of XPath (and most of XML) is still developing and has a long way to go in its evolution.

Table 6-3 shows a list of string functions and touches on the syntax and use of these functions. As always, refer to the official W3C specs for full details.

Table 6-3 String Functions

String Function	Description	Example
string **string(***object?***)**	Returns a string (as described earlier) from the object passed.	N/A
string **concat(***string, string, ..., string***)**	Concatenates arguments.	**concat(**"*a*", "*string*", "*to*", "*concatenate*"**)** yields astringtoconcatenate
boolean **starts-with(***string, string***)**	Returns true if first argument string starts with second argument string; else, returns false.	**starts-with(**"*string*", "*astringto-concatenate*"**)** returns true.
string **substring-before(***string, string***)**	Returns a substring of the *first* argument string that precedes the *first occurrence* of the *second argument* string contained in the *first* argument string or an empty string if it is not found in the second argument string.	**substring-before** ("*concatenate*", "*astringto-concatenate*") returns astringto.
string **substring-after(***string, string***)**	Returns a substring of the *first* argument string that follows the *first occurrence* of the *second* argument string contained in the *first* argument string or an empty string if it is not found in the second argument string.	**substring-after(**"*astringto*", "*astringto-concatenate*"**)** returns concatenate.
string **substring(***string, number, number?***)**	Returns a substring starting at the index of the second argument of length specified by the (optional) third argument. Omitting the final argument returns the entire string that follows the first argument.	**substring(**"*stringto-concatenate*", "*6*", "*6*"**)** returns concat; **substring** ("*astringto-concatenate*", "*6*") returns concatenate.

string **translate**(*string,* *string, string*)	Returns the first string with characters contained in the second string replaced by the characters in the same positions in the third string. This is a positional replacement, so characters in the third string may be repeated. If there is no corresponding character, based on position, in the third (replacement) string, then the character is removed. If a character in the first string is not found in the second, then it is ignored. The case of the replacement character is maintained.	**translate**("*a string* *to concatenate*", "*cat*", "*dog*") returns dondogenoge; **translate**("*a string* *to concatenate*", "*cat*", "*do*") returns dondoenoe.
string **normalize-** **space**(*string?*)	Returns the first string with leading and following white space stripped, as well as multiple spaces being replaced by a single space.	**normalize-space**("*a* *string to* *concatenate*") returns a string to concatenate.
boolean **contains**(*string,* *string*)	Returns true if first argument string contains second argument string; else, returns false.	**contains** ("*a string to* *concatenate*", "*string*") returns true; contains("*a string to* *concatenate*", "*house*") returns false.
number **string-** **length**(*string?*)	Returns the number of characters in the argument string. If the argument is omitted, it returns the number of characters in the context node.	N/A

Number functions include tools to determine the validity of an object as a number (as opposed to a string), to perform arithmetic and mathematical functions on numerical objects, and to determine or set ranges of values, as well as rounding and integer functions. Most of these are typical of the functions found in other languages, again, like the string functions, with most of them providing the

basic needs of document parsing and manipulation as opposed to powerful, eso-
teric mathematics.

The number functions for the most part accept a single argument, the value or
object that needs to be tested or manipulated. The only one that has an optional
object value is `number()`, which uses the context node being used as a default. A
list of the number functions, their arguments and return values, and a simple
example are shown in Table 6-4. As you can see, the list is fairly short but most
likely will continue to grow.

Table 6-4 Number Functions

Function	Description	Example
number **number** *(object?)*	Converts the value of the argument to a number. If a string contains a numerical value, that value is returned; otherwise, it is NaN. A Boolean `true` is converted to a 1; `false` is 0.	**number(**"*123 Sesame St*"**)** returns 123; **number(**"*Sesame St*"**)** returns NaN.
number **sum(***node-set***)**	Returns the sum for each node set in the argument node set or their converted string values.	N/A
number **floor** *(number)*	Returns the greatest integer for the argument that is not larger than the argument.	**floor**("*123.456*") returns 123.
number **ceiling** *(number)*	Returns the next highest integer for the argument that is not smaller than the argument.	**ceiling**("*123.456*") returns 124.
number **round** *(number)*	Returns the integer that is closest (<0.5) to the argument, either up or down to the next integer.	**round**("*123.456*") returns 123; **round**("*123.567*") returns 124.

Boolean functions return a true or false value based on the testing of the object
passed in as an argument. These are useful for logic comparisons as well as conditionals. The Boolean functions are shown in Table 6-5.

Table 6-5 Boolean Functions

Function	Description	Example
boolean **boolean**(object)	Returns the Boolean value of the object based on the following rules: A number object returns true if it is a nonzero number; otherwise, it returns false (for positive or negative zero or NaN)	**boolean**("*123.456*") returns true; **boolean**("*a string to concatenate*") returns false.
boolean **not**(*object*)	Returns true if object is false; otherwise, false.	**not**(**boolean**("*a string to concatenate*")) returns true.
boolean **true**()	Returns true; otherwise, false.	**true**() returns true.
boolean **false**(*object*)	Returns false; otherwise, true.	**false**() returns false.
boolean **lang**(*string*)	Returns true if the context node is the same as the language specified in the xml:lang attribute of the context node or, failing that, its nearest ancestor that does specify an xml:lang attribute; otherwise, false.	

6.4   Data Model

The XPath data model acts on the tree structure of the XML document and, as specified in XPath 1.0, provides a conceptual model with little implementation. The data model defined in XSL Transformations 2.0 also will be used in XPath 2.0 and in XQuery 1.0. This data model has a twofold purpose. First, it defines the information that can be contained in the input of an XSLT processor (which serves to transform XML into XHTML for display on a browser) or an XQuery processor (for querying an XML document for a certain piece of information that it may contain). Using the same data model for all three of these branches of XML allows you to create very intelligent and specific location searches or data queries based on the core function library and expressions discussed earlier.

The data model itself relies on the XML infoset with a few additional requirements. The most applicable new feature (to this discussion) is support for XML Schema types. Data in the data model fall into five types, or categories:

- Nodes
- Simple values
- Sequences
- Error
- Schema

The Nodes category is defined in the W3C specification as containing eight distinct node types:

- Document
- Element
- Attribute
- Text
- Namespace
- Processing instruction
- Comment
- Reference (added in XPath 2.0)

These will be familiar because they have been discussed throughout the text and will not require any redefinition, but a few clarifications may be in order. The document and element nodes may have child nodes, but the others cannot. Each node has (at most) one and only one parent node but may have several ancestors. The node that has no parent is considered to be the root node unless it's a namespace node, which does not have a parent. Element and attribute nodes have a typed value as per the schema or DTD definitions. The new node category is *reference,* which is intended to provide a reference to an arbitrary node and preserve its identity to be referenced at a later time.

Simple values are comprised of primitive values and derived values. A *primitive value* is a value contained in the collection of the 19 XML Schema datatypes (see the W3C at www.w3.org/TR/xmlschema-2/ for the full list). Some examples are xs:string, xs:boolean, xs:decimal, and xs:float. These are very similar to datatypes discussed earlier or those found in most programming languages. A few of the (perhaps) unusual types are xs:base64binary (a MIME type), xs:anyURI, xs:QName, and xs:NOTATION, which are specific to XML and the needs of XPath.

A *derived value* is made up of a primitive base type with a facet (such as a pattern) to constrain it. An example used in the W3C documentation is that of a stock keeping unit (SKU) for inventory purposes.

This is declared as

```
<simpleType name="SKU" base="string">
  <pattern value="\d{3}-[A-Z] {2}"/>
</simpleType>
```

The constructor for this example states that it is a `simpleType` based on the datatype `"string"` named `"SKU"` and we're looking for a value contained in the pattern declared. The corresponding datatype for the simple type must be a schema component. The constructor takes a primitive value and the type to create the simple type.

The model for the simple type looks like this:

- *Simple value.* `(PrimitiveValue, SchemaComponent) -> SimpleValue`
- *Value.* `SimpleValue -> PrimitiveValue`
- *Type.* `SimpleValue -> SchemaComponent`

which resolves to

- *Value.* `SimpleValue -> xs:string`

Sequences are part of the data model, so a list can be used to derive a base type for the simple type; however, the current model does not include key values or references even though the XML Schema does. Hopefully, this will be added in the future.

For now, however, we can use a flat list to store a sequence collection. The catch here is that the sequence cannot store other sequences but may contain duplicate nodes or simple values. Sequences do not have an identity per se but may be compared for equality using a value. The constructors for a sequence define the construction of an empty sequence, or append, which allows any number of values to be appended to the sequence.

The two sequence types are as follows:

- *Empty sequence.* `Sequence<UnitValue>`
- *Append.* `Sequence<UnitValue>,. . . , Sequence<UnitValue>`
  `->Sequence<UnitValue>`

The sequence has three *accessors* (or ways to access the values). The first is the *empty* accessor, which returns `true` if the argument passed is empty; otherwise, `false`. Next is the *head* accessor, which looks at the first value in a nonempty sequence and returns it. Finally, there is the *tail* accessor, which returns all items in a nonempty sequence.

These are modeled as follows:

- *Empty.* `Sequence<UnitValue>... -> xs:boolean`
- *Head.* `Sequence<UnitValue>... -> UnitValue`
- *Tail.* `Sequence<UnitValue>... -> Sequence<UnitValue>`

Note: Sequences will be replacing the node sets found in XPath 1.0 when XPath 2.0 is ratified.

The *error* category provides a mechanism for capturing an error value that allows identification of an error condition. Error cannot appear in the content of *any* node in the data model, nor may it appear in a sequence. The handling of an error is specific to the implementation or application.

Schema components are represented by four flavors of schema-component values:

- Element declaration
- Attribute declaration
- Simple type declaration
- Complex type declaration

Of these four types, the complex type declaration may need some definition; the others should be familiar. The *complex type definition* is made up of data that consists of elements, attributes, or element content (whereas the simple type is just character data).

The example provided by the W3C is the best so far:

```
<?xml version=1.0?>
<p:part xmlns:p="http://www.mywebsite.com/PartSchema"
      xs:schemaLocation =
      "http://www.mywebsite.com/PartSchema"
      name="nutbolt">
   <mfg>Acme</mfg>
   <price>10.50</price>
</p:part>
```

And the accompanying schema is

```
<xs:schema xmlns:xsd="http://www.w3.org/1999/XMLSchema"
   targetNamespace="http://www.mywebsite.com/PartSchema">
   <xs:element name="part" type="part-type">
     <xs:complexType name="part-type">
         <xs:element name = "mfg" type="xs:string"/>
         <xs:element name = "price" type="xs:decimal"/>
         <xs:attribute name = "name" type="xs:string"/>
     </xs:complexType>
   </xs:element>
</xs:schema>
```

On further inspection, the preceding code sample can be further reduced to the schema components. Follow the mapping of the components as A1, B1, and so on to get a sense of the underlying construction. This example is from the W3C's "XQuery 1.0 and XPath 2.0 Data Model, W3C Working Draft, 7 June 2001." Comments are presented as

```
// A Comment Here
   // Document node D1
   children(D1)     = E1
```

```
parent(D1)           = empty-sequence()

// Element node E1
name(E1)        = xfo:expanded-
    QName("http://www.mywebsite.com/PartSchema", "part")
children(E1)         = append(E2, E3)
attributes(E1)    = A1
namespaces(E1)    = N1
parent(E1)           = D1
declaration(E1)   = SC1

typed-valued(E1) = empty-sequence()
type(E1)             = SC2

// Attribte node A1
name(A1)        = xfo:QNAME(empty-sequence(), "name")
string-value(A1) = "nutbolt"
parent(A1)        = E1
declaration(A1)   = SC3

typed-value(A1)  = "nutbolt"
type(A1)             = SC4

// Namespace node N1
name(N1)             = xfo:expanded-QName(empty-sequence(),
                     "p")
uri(N1)              = xfo:anyURI("http://www.mywebsite.com/
    PartSchema")
parent(N1)           = E1

// Element node E2
name(E2)        = xfo:QNAME(empty-sequence(), "mfg")
children(E2)      = T1
attributes(E2)    = empty-sequence()
namespaces(E2)    = N1
parent(E2)        = E1
declaration(E2)   = SC5

typed-value(E2)  = simple-value("Acme", SC4)
type(E2)             = SC4

// Element node E3
name(E3)        = xfo:QNAME(empty-sequence(), "price")
children(E3)      = T2
attributes(E3)    = empty-sequence()
namespaces(E3)    = empty-sequence()
parent(E3)        = E1
declaration(E3)   = SC6

typed-value(E3)  = simple-value(10.50, SC7)
type(E3)             = SC7
```

```
// Text node T1
value(T1)          = "Acme"
parent(T1)         = E2

// Text node T2
value(T2)          = "10.50"
parent(T2)         = E3

// Schema component SC1
component-kind(SC1)          = "element-declaration"
name(SC1)                    = xfo:expanded-
    QName("http://www.mywebsite.com/PartSchema",
    "part")
parent(SC1)                  = empty-sequence()
base(SC1)                    = xs:AnyElement
derived-by-extension(SC1)    = false
derived-by-refinement(SC1)   = true

// Schema component SC2
component-kind(SC2)          = "type-definition"
name(SC2)                    = xfo:expanded-
    QName("http://www.mywebsite.com/PartSchema",
    "part-type")
parent(SC2)                  = SC1
base(SC2)                    = xs:AnyComplexType
derived-by-extension(SC2)    = false
derived-by-refinement(SC2)   = true

// Schema component SC3
component-kind(SC3)          = "attribute-declaration"
name(SC3)                    = xfo:expanded-
    QName("http://www.mywebsite.com/PartSchema",
    "name")
parent(SC3)                  = SC1
base(SC3)                    = xs:AnyAttribute
derived-by-extension(SC3)    = false
derived-by-refinement(SC3)   = true

// Schema component SC4
component-kind(SC4)          = "simple-type-definition"
name(SC4)                    = xfo:expanded-
    QName("http://www.w3.org/1999/XMLSchema", "string")
parent(SC4)                  = empty-sequence()
base(SC4)                    = xs:AnySimpleType
derived-by-extension(SC4)    = false
derived-by-refinement(SC4)   = true

// Schema component SC5
component-kind(SC5)          = "element-declaration"
name(SC5)                    = xfo:expanded-
    QName("http://www.mywebsite.com/PartSchema", "mfg")
```

```
parent(SC5)                 = SC2
base(SC5)                   = xs:AnyElement
derived-by-extension(SC5)   = false
derived-by-refinement(SC5)  = true

// Schema component SC6
component-kind(SC6)         = "element-declaration"
name(SC6)                   = xfo:expanded-
    QName("http://www.mywebsite.com/PartSchema",
    "price")
parent(SC6)                 = SC2
base(SC6)                   = xs:AnyElement
derived-by-extension(SC6)   = false
derived-by-refinement(SC6)  = true

// Schema component SC7
component-kind(SC7)         = "simple-type-definition"
name(SC7)                   = xfo:expanded-
    QName("http://www.w3.org/1999/XMLSchema",
    "decimal")
parent(SC7)                 = empty-sequence()
base(SC7)                   = xs:AnySimpleType
derived-by-extension(SC7)   = false
derived-by-refinement(SC7)  = true
```

One last note: In XPath 1.0, the data model defines only nodes, and the primitive types (number, Boolean, string, etc.) are part of the expression language, not the data model proper. This should change with XPath 2.0.

 Review Questions

6.1 The context referred to in location path consists of
   a. context node.
   b. context position and size.
   c. variable bindings.
   d. all of the above.
   e. none of the above.

6.2 Which of the following symbols are used in XPath?
   a. //
   b. ?
   c. \
   d. /
   e. .

6.3 Which of the following characters indicates *root*?

    a. //
    b. ?
    c. \
    d. /
    e. .

6.4 What is meant by *axes*?

    a. The relationship between the start and end of a document
    b. The relationship between nodes of a document
    c. The relationship between two documents

6.5 Name five axes used in XPath.

6.6 What does an expression consist of?

    a. Variable reference
    b. Function call
    c. Pointer
    d. Core

6.7 What are the four basic types of core functions?

6.8 Which of these are number functions?

    a. `int()`
    b. `concat()`
    c. `true()`
    d. `round()`

6.9 Is the data model the same for XPath 2.0 and XPath 1.0?

6.10 Is XML Schema a component of the data model?

Problems

Using Figure 6-7, identify the following using the node letter codes.

6.1   Child of `ccc`.
6.2   Descendants of `ccc`.
6.3   Parent of `ccc`.
6.4   Ancestors of `ccc`.
6.5   Siblings of `ccc`.
6.6   Following sibling of `ccc`.
6.7   Preceding sibling of `ccc`.
6.8   Following of `ccc`.
6.9   Preceding of `ccc`.
6.10 Self of `ccc`.
6.11 Descendant or self of `ccc`.
6.12 Ancestor or self of `ccc`.

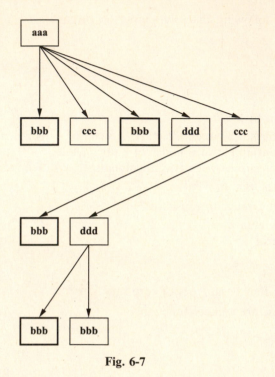

Fig. 6-7

 # Answers to Review Questions

6.1 d. all of the above. The context consists of a context node, a context position and size, variable bindings, and an initial context.

6.2 a, d, and **e**. The ? and \ are not part of the XPath syntax.

6.3 d. The / is the symbol for *root*.

6.4 b. Axes refer to the relationship between the nodes of a document.

6.5 The axes are child, descendant, parent, ancestor, sibling, following sibling, preceding sibling, following, preceding, self, descendent or self, and ancestor or self.

6.6 a and **b**. Variable reference and function call

6.7 Number, node set, Boolean, string

6.8 a, c, and **d**. int(), round(), and true() are Boolean, and concat() is a string function.

6.9 No, the data model for 1.0 is more conceptual in nature, and 2.0 is more implementable.

6.10 Yes, it is most important as of version XPath 2.0.

Solutions to Problems

6.1 ddd

6.2 ddd, bbb

6.3 aaa

6.4 aaa

6.5 bbb, ddd

6.6 bbb, ddd

6.7 bbb, ddd

6.8 ddd, bbb

6.9 aaa

6.10 ccc

6.11 ccc, ddd, bbb

6.12 ccc, aaa

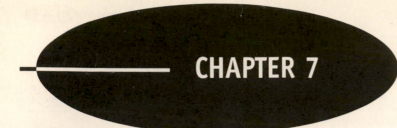

CHAPTER 7

XSL and XSLT

7.1   Use of XPath in XSLT

In earlier chapters, the Extensible Markup Language (XML) was presented as a content-driven markup language, and the Extensible Hypertext Markup Language (XHTML) was presented as a presentation-driven language. In Chapter 4, Cascading Style Sheets (CSS) and its application to XML was introduced. Now it is time to apply the presentation to the content.

The Extensible Stylesheet Language (XSL) is used to apply XML styling (that is, presentation) to XML. This is accomplished using the Extensible Stylesheet Language Transformations (XSLT), in which the XML is combined with CSS to create a document that can be rendered on a Web browser or other user agent (UA).

The process of styling requires an XML source document that contains the information to be displayed and a style sheet to define and describe how the document should be presented. In the XML document, there are processing instructions (PIs) that declare the XSL document to be used in CSS and its location or Uniform Resource Identifier (URI). The entire process is described more fully in subsequent sections of this chapter.

XPath is used by XSLT as a means to create a result tree from the source tree (the XML document) and the instruction tree of the XSLT document. Chapter 6 (XPath) discussed how a node can be specified, and by using XPath, the XML document tree may be traversed and subsections of the document may be accessed. XSLT uses XPath to specify where information is stored in the source (XML) file. Whereas before XPath was used to ascertain node context and relationships within the XML document, XPath is used again, but this time as notation from the XSLT file for styling information. Chapter 6 also described expressions such as child, parent, sibling, ancestor, and so on, along with some simple core functions to test portions of the document for location. In XSLT, the nodes are inspected for style attributes using the same tools.

This chapter uses core functions of XPath, as well as the `match/pattern` scenario to look for attributes such as `xsl:template`, `xsl:value-of` and the like. XPath allows XSLT to decide whether a given element or attribute appears in a given node or context.

7.2   The XSLT Transformation Process

The XSLT process consists of two main steps. The first is called *tree transformation*, and it takes the XML and XSL documents as input and generates a *result tree* based on the instructions contained in the XSL file. This might include filtering information (nodes to include or not include) or reordering XML data into a more presentable layout before applying the final style attributes at the time of rendering.

The complete series of steps involved includes

1. An XML parser interprets the XML document and forms a tree.
2. The tree is handed off to an XSLT processor.
3. The XSLT processor compares the nodes in the tree with the instructions contained in the referenced style sheet (XSL).
4. When the XSLT processor finds a match, it outputs a tree fragment (result tree).
5. The tree is output to a UA in a format such as the Hypertext Markup Language (HTML), speech, or text.

One of the key differences between CSS and XSL is that CSS uses rules to establish what is styled and how it is styled. XSL, on the other hand, uses templates that are associated with an XML element. An XSL template uses a `match` attribute to indicate the template needed (of which there can be several) and then creates a transformation from there.

The simple motion picture example from Chapter 2 lends itself to using an XSL style sheet and applying it for HTML output quite easily. Here is the XML:

```
<?xml version="1.0"?>
<?xml-stylesheet type="text/xsl" href="filmlibrary.xsl"?>
<filmlibrary>
<motionpicture>
    <title>"The Wizard of Oz"</title>
    <year>1939</year>
    <genre category="musical"></genre>
</motionpicture>
<motionpicture>
    <title>"Duck Soup"</title>
    <year>1933</year>
    <genre category="comedy"></genre>
</motionpicture>
<motionpicture>
    <title>"Gone With the Wind"</title>
    <year>1939</year>
    <genre category="drama"></genre>
</motionpicture>

</filmlibrary>
```

Next, create a transformation template as an XSL style sheet:

```
<?xml version="1.0"?>
<xsl:stylesheet xmlns:xsl="http://www.w3.org/TR/WD-xsl">
    <xsl:template match="/">
<html>
<head>
<title>Film Library</title>
</head>
    <body>
    <table border="2" bgcolor="white">
        <tr>
            <th>Title</th>
            <th>Genre</th>
            <th>Year</th>
        </tr>
<xsl:for-each select="filmlibrary/motionpicture">
        <tr>
            <td><xsl:value-of select="title"/></td>
            <td><xsl:value-of select="genre"/></td>
            <td><xsl:value-of select="year"/></td>
        </tr>
</xsl:for-each>
    </table>
    </body>
</html>
</xsl:template>
</xsl:stylesheet>
```

Look at the middle part of the XSL style sheet—except for the references to `<xsl:for-each select="filmlibrary/motionpicture">`—the code looks remarkably like plain old HTML. What we have here is a style template embedded in the HTML style document. When this `xsl:template` encounters an attribute named `title`, `genre`, or `year`, it captures the value and writes it to the HTML.

The trick is in the statement

```
<xsl:for-each select="filmlibrary/motionpicture">
.
.
.
</xsl:for-each>
```

This loops through the XML source tree, finds all the attributes possessing the sought-for names, and creates one row for each match. The loop runs until no more matches are found. Therefore, the table created here will have only three rows, but if the source file were a list of the 100 top films of the twentieth century, it then would contain 100 table rows.

The last step in this short example is to link the two files. This is accomplished with the PI

```
<?xml-stylesheet type="text/xsl" href="filmlibrary.xsl"?>
```

This statement assumes that the XSL file is called filmlibrary.xsl. Standard syntax for the URI path applies to XSL as well. Our final XML output then looks like Figure 7-1 (using Cooktop 2000, an excellent freeware editor).

Title	Genre	Year
"The Wizard of Oz"	Musical	1939
"Duck Soup"	Comedy	1933
"Gone With the Wind"	Drama	1939

Fig. 7-1.   XML output after applying an XSL style sheet for the motion picture example from Chapter 2.

Go back to the template and look at the for-each statement again. If we change the order of the searched elements, just in the XSL, it changes the entire formatting of the output.

In this example, year and genre are reversed. The XSL template is

```
<xsl:for-each select="filmlibrary/motionpicture">
<tr>
<td><xsl:value-of select="title"/></td>
<td><xsl:value-of select="year"/></td>
<td><xsl:value-of select="genre"/></td>
</tr>
</xsl:for-each>
```

The second result is shown in Figure 7-2.

7.3   XSLT Variable, Expressions, and Datatypes

Datatypes in XSL and XSLT are consistent with those found in the other languages of the XML family. The types are not strongly cast but, like JavaScript or other dynamically typed languages, are forgiving. The types listed in the XSL 1.0 W3C Recommendation are string, number, boolean, node-set, and tree. Each of these datatypes has been discussed before, but a short review might be in order.

```
- filmlibrary.xml :
```
| source (xml) | xpath console | stylesheet(xsl) | result | result(html) |

Title	Genre	Year
"The Wizard of Oz"	1939	Musical
"Duck Soup"	1933	Comedy
"Gone With the Wind"	1939	Drama

Fig. 7-2.   Reversing `year` and `genre` for the motion picture example.

- *String*. Characters (letters, numbers, etc.) that are not intended to be used in numeric or arithmetic calculations (although a string may be `eval()`'d). Any sequence of characters is allowed as a string in XML.

- *Number*. An integer or floating-point numeric value.

- *Boolean*. A true or false value.

- *Node set*. A set of nodes that can be found in the source tree.

- *Tree*. The root node and children of the result tree, as allowed in XSLT.

Variables are available in two flavors: global and local. *Global variables* are scoped to be available throughout an entire XSLT style sheet, but the *local variables* are limited to the template that creates them. The manner in which a variable is declared determines the variable's scope.

Variables are defined using the `<xsl:variable>` element, setting both the name of the variable and a select value; for example:

`<xsl:variable name="text_color" select="red">`

Every subsequent use of the `$text_color` variable provides the (string) value of `red`.

Now here's the scoping part of the variable defining process:

- If the `xsl:variable` element is used at the top level of the style sheet as a child (not just a descendant) of the `xsl:stylesheet` element, then it is scoped as a global variable.

- If it is declared within the `xsl:template` element, it is scoped as a local variable.

Thus, for variables that are needed globally, it is best to declare and initialize them at the beginning of the document using the `xsl:variable` immediately after the `xsl:stylesheet` element, even if the variable might not be called until much later in the document. Because datatyping is not critical, a reference to the variable name and an initial value (select) are all that are required. Be careful of reserved words, and follow standard, accepted naming practices.

Expressions in XSLT follow the syntax used in XPath. The use of an expression allows you to evaluate a variable or the context of a node. Expressions consist of a *variable reference,* which evaluates to the value bound to a variable name, or a *function call,* which calls a named function and allows the passing of arguments or testing of the context node as a default and returns a value.

In the case of a function call, the returned value datatype is based on the function, and an error may be returned if the chosen function is not appropriate. For example, a string value is returned from a string function, and a true or false is returned from a Boolean function type. If you try to interchange them, trouble (in the form of errors) is the guaranteed result. The Boolean is valuable when used with a conditional expression, such as equal to, greater or less than, or logical (such as not, and, or or) or combination of these, but not for string concatenation.

Another type of expression used in XSLT (and XPath) is the *pattern.* Patterns are a limited form of location path used to describe a step-by-step path needed to reach a desired node from the context node of a given element. The pattern comparison is an implied Boolean, returning `true` (a match) if the match is found and `false` (or empty) if it is not.

Using the combination of the attribute `match` (or `select`) and a value for a pattern allows a node to be compared for contextual validity and relative location in reference to the current node. A simple example based on an `/aaa/ccc` location path statement would be indicated as `match="/aaa/ccc"` or `select="/aaa/ccc"`. This specifies all elements `ccc` that are children of the root element `aaa`. The expression syntax defined in the preceding section also can be used in the `match/pattern` pair.

Patterns are allowed singularly or in combinations of multiple statements using the proper characters and syntax, such as the | to delineate alternates, and so on. Patterns frequently are used as values in a `select` attribute in XSL when they cannot be used as a `match` for node sets. This flexibility allows elements to be searched as paths or as a pattern match.

In practice, expressions are constructed of variables, conditionals, and functions. The characters used in expressions to define node context (and node sets) are shown in Table 7-1.

Table 7-1   Characters Used in
Expressions

Character	Description
/	Root node
//	Descendant (or self) node
.	Self node
..	Parent node

Additionally, XSLT uses the same axes as used in XPath, as follows (based on the current, or *context,* node):

- `child`. The children of the context node.
- `descendant`. All descendants.
- `parent`. The parent (or direct ancestor).
- `ancestor`. All ancestors between the root and the current parent node.
- `sibling`. Nodes with a shared parent.
- `following-sibling`. Siblings to the right of the context node.
- `preceding-sibling`. Siblings to the left of the context node.
- `following`. All following nodes in the document.
- `preceding`. All preceding nodes in the document.
- `self`. The context node itself.
- `descendant-or-self`. The context node and its descendant.
- `ancestor-or-self`. The context node and its ancestor.

Here are some key points to remember:

- Datatypes are dynamic, not strongly cast.
- Variables are declarative (cannot be updated).
- Variables are local or global depending on when (and where) they are defined.
- Expressions use XPath syntax.
- Core functions are used in the same manner as in XPath, with the same syntax and datatype restraints.

7.4　Structure of XSL Style Sheets

A style sheet is (usually) intended to provide the markup needed to present a document, whether it is intended for a Web browser, personal digital assistant (PDA), or text-to-speech device. The structure of the style sheet is based on the three main elements of a presentable document:

- Content
- Layout
- Style

The content, of course, is contained in the XML document, which will be used to generate the source tree and will be validated by the XML parser, but the quality of the content itself is left up to you. As is always the case in XML, the content is stored and accessed independently of any presentation markup. Extra attention paid to maintaining clean, clear XML content will pay off when the time comes to transform the document. Keep the content/presentation relationship as pure as possible, even though the temptation may be there to do otherwise.

The layout can best be described as the way that the information is presented to the viewer or user agent, how the content is organized, as well as how the document flows. This step is critical and requires a good amount of thought for anything beyond a simple, dry text document. At this point, content and presentation begin to merge to form the output document. The transition is not yet complete, but elements of both are now present at the XSL processor, and the trees are being formed. Remember that the transformation style sheet only contains presentation instructions and that the content may change based on the XML file being transformed; in other words, the style sheet is still somewhat of a moving target.

Finally, the style of the layout should be considered, embracing such aspects as font style, color schemes, highlighting, tables, layers, and so on. At this point, CSS can be applied in addition to the XSL, or based on the UA, any number of stylistic touches may be applied to the document. This process has finally produced what is closest to a familiar HTML document, and it may be treated as such. Many XML practitioners will still leave the styling to CSS—the choice is yours.

Look again at (an abbreviated version of) the style sheet used earlier. Only the XSL elements are preserved:

```
<?xml version="1.0"?>
<xsl:stylesheet xmlns:xsl="http://www.w3.org/TR/WD-xsl">
    <xsl:template match="/">
        <xsl:for-each select="filmlibrary/motionpicture">
            <xsl:value-of select="title"/>
            <xsl:value-of select="genre"/>
            <xsl:value-of select="year"/>
        </xsl:for-each>
    </xsl:template>
</xsl:stylesheet>
```

All these elements are addressed in the style sheets that are called from the XML document source tree and fed into the XSL processor. Once the source file has been parsed and validated, the source tree is generated, and the structure of the XSL style sheet is parsed, with instructions for layout and style being added to the transition tree for output to the user agent.

The structure of the style sheet begins with a module that is identified by a PI in the source document that states `<?xml-stylesheet?>`. This is sometimes referred to as a *principal style sheet module*. From this module, other style sheet modules may be included by the statement `xsl:include` or `xsl:import`, and these in turn may `include` (or `import`) other modules, and on down the line it goes. Both of these extend the style sheet tree of the document.

The `xsl:include` element is essential to locating the XSLT document so that the appropriate transformations may be applied. Generally, the `xsl:include` element has this syntax, which follows established practice for the URI:

```
<xsl:include href="http://www.document.org">
```

This directive acts very much like an include file in a language such as C, C++, or Java.

The `xsl:import` element is intended to provide the means to import one style sheet module into another and allows style sheets to override each other.

The major difference between these two elements is that the `xsl:import` element is only allowed as a top-level element. In XSL Transformations (XSLT) version 1.0 (`www.w3.org/TR/xslt#import`), the W3C states:

> . . . the `xsl:import` element children must precede all other element children of an `xsl:stylesheet` element, including any `xsl:include` element children. When `xsl:include` is used to include a style sheet, any `xsl:import` elements in the included document are moved up in the including document to after any existing `xsl:import` elements in the including document. . . .

This simply means that `xsl:import` is declared before any other child elements (such as `xsl:include`) and that when `xsl:include` is used, any `xsl:import` elements of the included document are moved up to a position following the `xsl:import` of the including (original) document. You need to be sure this does not cause conflicts (your parser will let you know). If you are using `include` and `import`, the overall structure of the XSL/XML document will become more sensitive to element ordering, and it is important to pay special attention to the hierarchy of the elements in the document. Errors cannot be overlooked; they should be attended to because they have a way of presenting your document in the most hideous fashion when you least expect it.

7.5 Comparison of XSL and CSS

Although the goals of both XSL and CSS have common roots and on the surface they appear to accomplish the same result, the power of XSL becomes evident as search patterns become more complex. Although CSS provides some pattern searching, it primarily applies styles to elements and defines rules for the desired rendering of the XML document. CSS generally is thought of as being applicable mainly to HTML (or XHTML), whereas XSL is focused on XML.

CSS and XSLT are very complementary technologies as opposed to competing ones. Each still has a very prominent place in the XML world. Remember that CSS is a rules-based tool, whereas XSLT is template-based and, as such, can go well beyond simple styling to offer transformations, manipulations, and organization. However, bear in mind that frequently CSS will fit the bill quite nicely when XSLT would be considered overkill. Often HTML authors are more comfortable with CSS, whereas server-side folks (Structured Query Language, or SQL, and scripting types) may prefer XSLT. The choice depends on the circumstances and your preferences.

XSL is the more manipulative and dynamic of the two techniques and performs three primary tasks:

- It transforms an XML document.
- It defines the parts and patterns of an XML document.
- It formats an XML document.

Comparatively, CSS2 does the following:

- It provides selectors for pattern matching.
- It generates a formatting structure based on media type.
- It presents the document based on the UA.
- It transfers the formatting structure to the document tree.

At their most basic common denominators, both XSL and CSS can apply the presentation markup required by a UA to the document source file—whether it is XML or HTML. CSS provides some tools for pattern matching, such as element selection, but XSL surpasses CSS by providing much more complex possibilities. For example, an XSL pattern can select a fragment of a structure, such as the second item of a bulleted list or the sibling of a node for specific style application. CSS would have to accept the entire bulleted list as a selector for the style. Additionally, there are comparative operators and the like available in XSL that can test an element and its contents to determine the validity of the selector.

Whereas CSS properties allow you to specify a wide range of characteristics for display and rendering of an element, XSL goes beyond decoration to actually interacting with the document structure and provides the necessary formatting and style that the document requires.

Transformation through XSL is accomplished by joining a source document (XML) with an XSL document. The source tree of the XML document is combined with the style tree of the XSL file, and a result tree is produced.

XSL and CSS share a common goal: the application of styling information that is required for document rendering. How this goal is accomplished by the two languages is a bit divergent. CSS uses selectors to indicate the element that is being styled, and each selector provides properties of the style. The syntax for the CSS selector is as follows:

```
selector{property_1; property_2; ... ; property_n}
```

The selector is (usually) a standard HTML element such as p or table. In the case of XML, the user-defined (rather the DTD- or schema-defined) elements are indicated as the selector. Either way works just fine. The properties listed in the selector must be values that the UA can interpret and apply. In the case of a heading color style, it makes the most sense to use either a numeric red-green-blue (RGB) color value or choose from a standardized color list. (See www.w3.org/TR/html4/types.html#h-6.5 for the 16 main color names and their corresponding RGB values.) Here is an example of a heading color style:

```
h1 { color:red }
```

Sizes and weights are number-based (and there are a lot of units to choose from), so there is less margin for misinterpretation than there is with colors. Refer to Chapter 4 for more detail.

XSL uses a different system, which is made up of pattern matching and formatting objects that look like the following (notice that all rules for XML well-formedness apply to XSL just as with any other XML element):

```
<xsl:template match="pattern goes here">
<formatting object(s) go here />
</xsl:template>
```

XSL applies styles by incorporating XPath into the `pattern` statement to indicate which element(s) are to receive the style (as a selector) and formatting object as the properties to be applied to those elements.

The style example used before would look like this in XSL:

```
<xsl:template match="h1">
    <fo:block color="red">
        <xsl:apply-templates/>
    </fo:block>
</xsl:template>
```

On the surface this looks wordy and perhaps a bit confusing, but when all the complexity of XSL is taken into consideration, the thoroughness of the `xsl:template` makes sense. For example, elements can be reordered or replaced via regular expressions. Elements can be counted and, based on their positioning, can receive a certain style application. The use of formatting objects will be explored more thoroughly later in this chapter.

7.6   XSLT Top-Level Elements

A top-level element in XSLT is any element that can occur as a child to the `xsl:stylesheet` (or its synonym `xsl:transform`) element. The following 12 elements in XSLT are top-level elements:

- `xsl:attribute-set`
- `xsl:decimal-format`
- `xsl:import`
- `xsl:include`
- `xsl:key`
- `xsl:namespace-alias`
- `xsl:output`
- `xsl:param`
- `xsl:preserve-space`
- `xsl:strip-space`
- `xsl:template`
- `xsl:variable`

These are the only elements that `xsl:stylesheet` (`xsl:transform`) can contain. A style sheet is represented by the `xsl:stylesheet` element and must contain the `version` attribute. All other elements are optional.

The bare-bones style sheet declaration is

```
<xsl:stylesheet version="number">
.
.
.
</xsl:stylesheet>
```

Typically, more complete information is included, such as in this example from XSL Transformations (XSLT) version 1.0, published by the W3C (www.w3.org/TR/xslt#stylesheet-element):

```
<xsl:stylesheet version="1.0"
    xmlns:xsl="http://www.w3.org/1999/XSL/Transform">
      <xsl:import href="..."/>
      <xsl:include href="..."/>
      <xsl:strip-space elements="..."/>
      <xsl:preserve-space elements="..."/>
      <xsl:output method="..."/>
      <xsl:key name="..." match="..." use="..."/>
      <xsl:decimal-format name="..."/>
      <xsl:namespace-alias stylesheet-prefix="..."
      result-prefix="..."/>
      <xsl:attribute-set name="...">
       .
       .
       .
      </xsl:attribute-set>
      <xsl:variable name="...">...</xsl:variable>
      <xsl:param name="...">...</xsl:param>
      <xsl:template match="...">
       .
       .
       .
      </xsl:template>
      <xsl:template name="...">
       .
       .
       .
      </xsl:template>
</xsl:stylesheet>
```

The ellipses indicate where the content would go, and again, these are all optional elements, but remember that the xsl:stylesheet element must have the version attribute.

Furthermore, the order in which these elements appear in the document is not critical, with the exception of an import or include statement, which must be included before any elements it contains might be called.

7.7 Simplified XSLT

At the simplest level, the XSLT process may be viewed as nothing more than converting XML to HTML (or XHTML). Of course, XSLT goes well beyond just this conversion step, but to reduce it to its essence, we cover what XSLT does in this section.

The transformation of XML via the application of style sheets to form (X)HTML is a crucial and critical step to getting XML documents to the Web-browsing masses so that XML can establish a greater foothold in the markup universe. If the XML is not transformed properly and breaks down at the rendering stage, XML could remain an experimental good idea, and (X)HTML (and the myriad proprietary browser extensions) could remain dominant—pushing us further from our goal of compliance and smaller browsers. This becomes more evident in the world of handheld devices, cellular phones, PDAs, and so on because application size is of the essence, and the ability to tailor renderings (content plus presentation) to UAs becomes more important.

Remember that XSL provides formatting objects (that is, instructions) to an XSLT processor (such as Xalan from the Apache group—`http://xml.apache.org/`), where they are applied to the XML source tree, creating a document that is served to the client UA as (X)HTML. As far as the UA is concerned (Web browser or PDA), HTML is HTML (or XHTML) whether produced at run time by an XSLT processor or a static HTTP server. The XSLT process is transparent to the end user, and because it is (usually) a process that is interpreted at the server on the fly, the dynamic document-generation possibilities are tremendous. Specifying the style required via the XSL file allows you to provide the optimal document for a given situation.

The simplified process looks something like that shown in Figure 7-3.

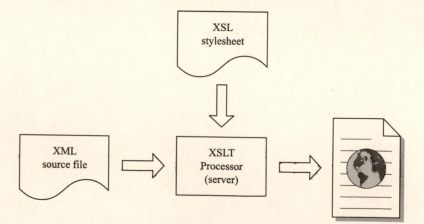

Fig. 7-3. **The process of applying an XSL style sheet.**

The steps involved in this simplified process are

1. Accepting an XML document
2. Accepting an XSL style sheet

3. Creating a result tree from the XML source tree
4. Interpreting the result tree
5. Formatting the output to the UA

The initial part of the process is called *tree transformation* (up through interpreting the result tree on the preceding list), and the rest of the process is called *formatting*. The actual formatter might be on the UA, where the XSL processor itself (the tree transformation) resides server side, as part of a greater XML serving application.

During the tree-transformation steps, the structure of the result tree can be modified quite a bit from the initial source tree to produce an output that is very different from where it started. For example, the content can be arranged differently in the result tree from the original document either by filtering or reordering the elements, again based on need. The formatting is applied to the result tree, not the source tree, so one can work within the legal range of modification and then apply the formatting. If you think about this for a moment, it should become apparent how versatile the documents can become.

Take the example of a quiz being contained as an XML document. It might contain 300 questions with answers. If each student group requires 50 questions (and no answers), it is easy to create a result tree of six complete sets of 50 questions each (filtering by node position), leaving out the answers on the student version and including the answers on the instructor's version. After the tree-transformation process produces the appropriate set of questions and version, the style is applied for formatting.

If this quiz is to be taken in the classroom, formatting can be applied that is appropriate for paper output. If it is a course delivered over the Web, the proper formatting for (X)HTML may be applied. Another possibility is that the quiz may be given to students who may suffer a visual impairment or some other special need, so formatting for voice output can be provided. All these possibilities are based on the original XML document, and all the output versions are provided by a simple XSL transformation.

Another possibility is to send both the XML document and the XSLT document to the browser and let the browser do the formatting work. This technique is more along the lines of the CSS method of presentation and depends on the capabilities of the XML rendering engine of the browser. In early 2002, XML support in browsers was limited and rather sparse, so for most documents, server-side formatting was the best option. This could change in late 2002, however, and is another way to shift some of the processing load from server to client. However, there is a bandwidth tradeoff between providing all the files to the client versus only what is required to present the document. Most likely, a middle-ground approach should be taken, sharing load and bandwidth. If multiple XML source documents can share a single XSLT file, it might be most efficient to have the formatting done on the browser (client) side. In the case of PDAs and other small devices, it is more efficient to do the formatting on the server. Ideally, either method should yield the same results, with the XSLT file being central to the success of the document presentation.

7.8 XSLT Template Bodies

XSL and XSLT use templates to describe how an XML document should be transformed for presentation. Whereas CSS uses selectors to apply style, XSL uses a `match` or `pattern` attribute to designate a style association with a particular document or portion of a document.

Taking a snippet of the style sheet markup used earlier in this chapter, the template portion is as follows:

```
<xsl:template match="/">
<xsl:for-each select="filmlibrary/motionpicture">
    <xsl:value-of select="title"/>
    <xsl:value-of select="genre"/>
    <xsl:value-of select="year"/>
</xsl:for-each>
</xsl:template>
```

As you can see, the template is defined as looking to match the / (root) character (in other words, the whole document), selecting (`for-each` as a loop) the nodes `filmlibrary/motionpicture` and then selecting from those the nodes `title`, `genre`, and `year` and applying the style to those nodes until the loop ends. Now, we did cut out the `table` elements to make the example clearer, but if they are returned, the styling becomes more apparent. The code loops through as instructed and uses the value found in the instructed node as a dynamic value to be embedded into or styled by (X)HTML.

Here is the entire style sheet, templates and all:

```
<?xml version="1.0"?>
<xsl:stylesheet xmlns:xsl="http://www.w3.org/TR/WD-xsl">
<xsl:template match="/">
<html>
<head>
<title>Film Library</title>
</head>
    <body>
    <table border="2" bgcolor="white">
        <tr>
            <th>Title</th>
            <th>Genre</th>
            <th>Year</th>
        </tr>
    <xsl:for-each select="filmlibrary/motionpicture">
        <tr>
            <td><xsl:value-of select="title"/></td>
            <td><xsl:value-of select="genre"/></td>
            <td><xsl:value-of select="year"/></td>
        </tr>
```

```
    </xsl:for-each>
</table>
</body>
</html>
</xsl:template>
</xsl:stylesheet>
```

If the template markup is removed, only style markup is left. Multiple templates can be created and used within the same style sheet, either in-line or using include and import, as discussed previously.

7.9   Attribute Value Templates

One method for adding new elements and attributes at the XSL stage (for output) is through attribute value templates. These templates allow you to convert between attribute and element (and vice versa) or supply either of these with a value derived from a function call or hard-coded statement (such as an SQL statement).

Because the main job of an XSLT processor is to follow the instructions found in the XSLT file, it has a handy access to the result tree as it is being created from the source tree of the XML file and the XSLT style sheet. Templates provide a means to insert values dynamically based on the document flow.

A common syntax for an attribute value template is as follows:

```
<xsl:stylesheet
     xmlns:xsl="http://www.w3.org/1999/XSL/Transform"
     version="1.0">
<xsl:template match="filmlibrary">
   <motionpicture>
      <title>The Wizard of Oz</title>
      <year><xsl:value-of select="/year"/></year>
      <xsl:apply-templates/>
   </motionpicture>
</xsl:template>
</xsl:stylesheet>
```

When the processor sees a filmlibrary element, it adds the xsl:apply-templates instruction and outputs the contents of the element by applying the motionpicture element, in essence renaming the filmlibrary element to motionpicture. However, before the motionpicture element is closed, two child elements are output, namely, title and year. In this case (of our example), the title (The Wizard of Oz) is hard coded, but the year is output via the xsl:value-of element that selects the value of the year element and uses that for the result.

To add attributes to an XML element through XSLT, a style sheet like the following can be used:

```
<xsl:stylesheet
       xmlns:xsl="http://www.w3.org/1999/XSL/Transform"
       version="1.0">
.
.
.

<xsl:template match="title">
   <title lead_actor="Frank Morgan" lead_actress="Judy
       Garland"
       director="Victor Fleming">
</xsl:template>
.
.
.

</xsl:stylesheet>
```

This would add three attributes (lead_actor, lead_actress, and director) and output a result of

```
<?xml version="1.0"?>
<motionpicture>
   <title lead_actor="Frank Morgan" lead_actress="Judy
       Garland"
       director="Victor Fleming">
       The Wizard of Oz
   </title>
.
.
.

</motionpicture>
```

Notice that the attributes we have used are hard coded. If a function return value or other variable were desired, we would use {@*something*} to capture the attribute value; for example, adding runtime as an attribute:

```
<xsl:stylesheet
       xmlns:xsl="http://www.w3.org/1999/XSL/Transform"
       version="1.0">
<xsl:template match="title">
<title lead_actor="Frank Morgan" lead_actress="Judy Garland"
       director="Victor Fleming" runtime="{@Runtime}">
</xsl:template>
</xsl:stylesheet>
```

The @Runtime variable is the value of the runtime attribute found in the title element. In the earlier example, the statement <xsl:value-of select="/year"/> indicates that the element year is to be selected, based on the / character. The @ indicates an attribute, and / indicates an element.

Values also can be inserted that are results of a function, such as `sibling()`, `parent()`, `position()`, and so on. The syntax for this is as follows:

```
<xsl:attribute name="dad">
    <xsl:value-of select="parent()"/>
</xsl:attribute>
```

7.10 XSLT and White Space

In the case of XSLT, white space stripping follows the construction of a tree from the source document or style sheet but before processing by the XSLT processor. White space is considered a text node and therefore is removed from the tree during stripping, but only if it contains nothing but white space. During the stripping steps, a set of element names in which white space must be preserved is input into the XSLT processor, and those elements are preserved untouched. This applies to both style sheet and source documents, but the actual set of preservation element names is specified separately.

Any unprotected nodes can be stripped, unless any of the following apply (from the W3C at `www.w3.org/TR/xslt#strip`):

- The element name of the parent of the text node is in the set of white space–preserving element names.

- The text node contains at least one non-white space character. As in XML, a white space character is #x20, #x9, #xD, or #xA.

- An ancestor element of the text node has an `xml:space` attribute with a value of `preserve`, and no closer ancestor element has `xml:space` with a value of default.

If none of these conditions apply, the text node containing the white space is stripped. For source documents (the XML file), the top-level elements `xsl:strip-space` and `xsl:preserve-space` specify the set(s) of preserved elements. Each of these has an `elements` attribute that has a list of white space–separated element names as its value, referred to as `NameTests`. The set of element names in `xsl:preserve-space` contains all the element names as an initial condition, but they are removed from the set if an element matches a `NameTest` on the `xsl:strip-space` list. The reverse is also true. If an element matches a `NameTest` on `xsl:preserve-space`, it is removed from `xsl:strip-space`. In the case of conflicts, the W3C has set up a series of tie breakers on its Web site at `www.w3.org/TR/xslt#conflict`.

7.11 Extending XSLT

The current XSLT specification contains two kinds of extensions: extension elements and extension functions. Extension elements serve as a means to specify namespaces as extension namespaces. If the XSLT processor encounters an element contained in the extended namespace, it treats the element as an instruction instead of a literal result element. Remember that this is after XML parsing and at the tree-transformation stage. The namespace that contains the element provides the semantics of the element and the instructions it imparts.

Extending XSLT allows a developer to create mechanisms for the transformation to go beyond its original intent and provides the means for elements to be replaced; for example, the `credit_card_number` element being replaced by the `EncryptedData` element with a localized change of just the XSLT style sheet. This capability also allows certain subsets of the document to be extended for specific users or UAs and gives the developer the freedom to further tailor the style sheet to his or her specific needs.

7.12   About XSL Formatting Objects

XSL formatting objects (sometimes abbreviated as XSL-FOs) are key components of XSL and XSLT, much like selectors are in CSS. Formatting objects are the second main portion of the XSL specification, intended to provide formatting semantics to XML objects during style transformations.

The syntax for XSL-FOs is fairly straightforward, reminiscent of the other XML languages and defined, as usual, at the W3C Web site (`www.w3.org/TR/xsl/slice6.html#fo-section`). XSL-FOs provide the vocabulary needed to describe layout, styling, and other presentation markup in great detail while remaining separate from the XML source. Formatting objects are applied during XSLT processing, and even though they can be very complex and verbose at times, the syntactical rules will be familiar to you by now.

In addition to (simple) formatting objects, FOP is available from Apache. FOP is intended primarily for the printing output of documents—hence the *P* at the end of the acronym. Frequently, the output is a PDF document, but most of the concepts between FO and FOP are similar.

Like all XML documents, the XSL-FO file begins with an XML declaration and root element:

```
<?xml version="1.0" encoding="utf-8"?>
<fo:root>
.
.
.
</fo:root>
```

Following this initial declaration is the remainder of the XSL-FO file, which consists of

- A master set for the layout, made up of
  - Descriptions of the kind of pages to be found in the document
  - The sequencing of the formats used in those pages

- The pages themselves

The master set for the document layout is a series of XSL-FO elements starting with the `fo:layout-master-set` element immediately after the `fo:root` element. The model for XSL-FO is based on the concept of areas, which are collections of rectangular regions that contain the text, images, white space, and other layout components. There are more than 50 elements associated with formatting objects, and each of them is based on the areas model.

The formatting objects differ primarily in the type of content they are meant to represent, whether it is a block of text, a list, or a table.

The XSL-FO areas are composed of these main groups (see `www.w3.org/TR/xsl/slice6.html#fo-section`):

- Declaration, pagination, and layout formatting objects
- Block formatting objects
- In-line formatting objects
- Table formatting objects
- List formatting objects
- Link and multiformatting objects
- Out-of-line formatting objects
- Other formatting objects

A document (and the master set) is made up of collections of these areas and objects that ultimately describe the page. The full list of XSL-FO elements can be found at the W3C Web site (again, see `www.w3.org/TR/xsl/slice6.html#fo-section`), but some of the common ones are

- `fo:block` defines a block region, similar to XHTML's `blockquote`.
- `fo:flow` contains the flowing text object that becomes pages.
- `fo:initial-property-set` specifies formatting properties for the first line of an `fo:block`.
- `fo:inline` is used for formatting a portion of text with a background or enclosing it within a border.
- `fo:layout-master-set` is the main wrapper for all master elements.
- `fo:page-sequence-master` specifies sequences of page masters that are used when generating pages.
- `fo:region-body` specifies the area located in the center of the `fo:simple-page-master` region.
- `fo:root` is the top node of an XSL result tree of formatting objects.
- `fo:simple-page-master` is used in the generation of pages and specifies the geometry of the page.

Of course, there are many tags, each of which is intended to provide specific formatting and style. An example of the use and syntax of the FO, modified from the W3C XSL Recommendation (at www.w3.org/TR/xsl/slice6.html# section-N13277-Inline-level-Formatting-Objects) should help:

```
<text>
<p>This is the text of a paragraph that is going to be presented with the first line in small-caps.</p>
</text>
```

And the XSL style sheet, keying on the p element, is

```
<?xml version="1.0"?>
<xsl:stylesheet
      xmlns:xsl="http://www.w3.org/1999/XSL/Transform"
      xmlns:fo="http://www.w3.org/1999/XSL/Format"
      version="1.0">
<xsl:template match="p">
   <fo:block>
        <fo:initial-property-set font-variant="small-caps"/>
        <xsl:apply-templates/>
   </fo:block>
</xsl:template>

</xsl:stylesheet>
```

And this derives the result tree instance:

```
<fo:block>
   <fo:initial-property-set font-variant="small-caps">
   </fo:initial-property-set>This is the text of a paragraph
        that is going to be presented with the first line in
        small-caps.
</fo:block>
```

 # Review Questions

7.1 What are the three trees used in XSL Transformations?
   a. Source tree
   b. Result tree
   c. Instruction tree
   d. Information tree
7.2 Put these steps in the correct order.
   a. A tree is handed off to an XSLT processor.
   b. The tree is output to a UA in a format such as HTML, speech, or text.

c. An XML parser interprets the provided XML document and forms a tree.

    d. When the XSLT processor finds a match, it outputs a tree fragment (result tree).

    e. The XSLT processor compares the nodes in the tree with the instructions contained in the referenced style sheet (XSL).

7.3 Which of the following does CSS use to establish what receives styling?

    a. Rules

    b. XPath

    c. Templates

    d. Tags

7.4 Which of the following does XSL use to establish what receives styling?

    a. Rules

    b. XPath

    c. Templates

    d. Tags

7.5 What must the style sheet declaration be included in?

    a. The XML source document

    b. The directory tree

    c. The CSS file

    d. The output file

7.6 Which of the following are advantages that XSL offers over CSS?

    a. Document manipulation

    b. Convenience

    c. Defines parts of a document

    d. Formats a document

7.7 Name four datatypes used in XSL and XSLT.

7.8 XSL and XSLT datatypes are strongly cast. True or false?

7.9 Which of the following are expressions in XSL?

    a. Pattern

    b. Function call

    c. Match

    d. Select

    e. All of the above

7.10 These are all FOs. True or false?

- Declaration, pagination, and layout formatting objects
- Block formatting objects
- In-line formatting objects
- Table formatting objects
- List formatting objects
- Link and multiformatting objects
- Out-of-line formatting objects
- Other formatting objects

Problem

Using the template example from before in Section 7.2, "The XSLT Transformation Process," create the changes needed to sort the fields

    a. Left to right as year, genre, and title.

    b. In order by year (descending) and title (alphabetical).

Here is the style sheet used before:

```
<?xml version="1.0"?>
<xsl:stylesheet xmlns:xsl="http://www.w3.org/TR/WD-xsl">
    <xsl:template match="/">
<html>
<head>
<title>Film Library</title>
</head>
    <body>
    <table border="2" bgcolor="white">
        <tr>
            <th>Title</th>
            <th>Genre</th>
            <th>Year</th>
        </tr>
<xsl:for-each select="filmlibrary/motionpicture">
        <tr>
            <td><xsl:value-of select="title"/></td>
            <td><xsl:value-of select="genre"/></td>
            <td><xsl:value-of select="year"/></td>
        </tr>
</xsl:for-each>
    </table>
    </body>
</html>
</xsl:template>
</xsl:stylesheet>
```

Answers to Review Questions

7.1 a, b, and c

7.2 The correct order is c, a, e, d, and b.

7.3 **a**. CSS uses rules to define styling.

7.4 **c**. XSL uses templates to define styling.

7.5 a

7.6 a, c, and d

7.7 The most common datatypes used in XSL and XSLT are

- String
- Number
- Boolean
- Node set
- Tree

7.8 False

7.9 e

7.10 True

CHAPTER 8

XLink, XPointer, and XBase

8.1   Use of XPath in XPointer

XPointer is a member of the Extensible Markup Language (XML) family that is built on top of the XML Path Language (XPath), which in turn is the expression language on which XSL Transformations (XSLT) is based. XPointer offers extensions to XPath that define addressing schemes, such as

- Locate information through *string matching*.
- Define address *points* and *ranges*.
- Define address *nodes*.
- Use XPath in Uniform Resource Identifier (URI) references to locate *addresses*.

XPointer is not designed to address the internal structure of the Document Type Definition (DTD) of an XML resource, even though it is intended to address fragments of an XML document. XPointer version 1.0 is defined to be a fragment identifier for the following media types:

- `text/xml`
- `application/xml`
- `text/xml-external-parsed-entity`
- `application//xml-external-parsed-entity`

Because schemas are XML documents, the limitations of scope for XPointer that affect the DTD should not be an issue. Reviewing key points of XPath (from Chapter 6) that apply to XPointer, it is obvious that XPath, by virtue of it being the underlying language of XPointer, plays a major role in the declaration of XPointer statements and resource identification.

The key points of XPath are as follows:

- The simple design goal for XPath is that it is a mechanism to identify and access portions or subsets of XML documents.

- XPath uses a path-based syntax that is similar to other traversal syntax used in file systems or document retrieval.

- XPath is a direct result of the needs of addressing used in XPointer and pattern matching used in XSLT.

- XPath provides a common foundation for solving a fundamental problem: the need to locate elements, attributes, and other XML document nodes in a concise and convenient way.

These goals form the basic premise for XPointer, particularly the ability to identify and access portions of an XML document. XPointer uses the XPath model of identifying nodes, as well as string pattern matching. XPointer extends XPath in a number of ways without negating any of the XPath functionality and syntax.

Extensions in XPointer add the following to XPath (derived from a list at www.w3.org/TR/WD-xptr#b2d250b5b9):

- Two new location types, namely, `point` and `range`. These correspond to Document Object Model (DOM) positions and ranges (see Chapter 5).

- A generalization of the in-place XPath concepts of nodes, node types, and node sets. These are added to the locations concept of XPointer.

- Rules for an XPath evaluation context.

- The functions `string-range()`, `range()`, and `range-to()`; `here()` and `origin()`; and `start-point()` and `end-point()`.

These extensions add the extra dimensions needed to create a framework for true document fragment accessibility, offering a powerful set of tools and methods to XML (and ultimately) the Web. The terms used in XPath and XPointer as components of the location paths and sets are

- `location`. A generalized node including points and ranges.

- `location-set`. An unordered list of locations.

- `sub-resource`. The actual portion of the XML document that is identified by XPointer.

- `arc`. The set of rules for traversing resources, lumped into a single entity.

- `axes` or `axis`. A sequence of nodes, including

  - `child`
  - `parent`
  - `self`
  - `ancestor`
  - `ancestor-or-self`
  - `attribute`
  - `descendant`

- `descendant-or-self`
- `following`
- `following-sibling`
- `namespace`
- `preceding`
- `preceding-sibling`

- `predicates`. Test for various criteria, such as the value of an attribute, returning a value such as Boolean `true` or `false`, `string`, or `number`.
- `functions`. Accept arguments and return results based on location sets or points that they contain, such as
  - `id()`
  - `here()`
  - `origin()`

The role of XPath in XPointer is to provide the tools and methods to locate resources as a subset of the nodes within the XML document. This is accomplished by filtering axis output by predicate. A node is inspected, following the declared axes, comparing the predicate attribute's value with the value of the node set, and returning the result.

XPath works on data sets that are derived from the markup and elements contained in the XML document. XPointer adds to this data set by identifying document fragments. XPointer accomplishes this using node traversal in an iterative mode, basing the subsequent traversal step on the prior step.

8.2   Using XPointers

Because XPointer extends XPath, most of the XPath concepts and methods carry over into XPointer. There are, of course, small and subtle differences, as one would expect, but for the most part, XPointer will be familiar in scope and syntax. The conditions in which XPointer should be applied are in cases such as the following:

- Using string matching to locate information
- Appending URIs for added flexibility and versatility to links
- Addressing a portion of a document node instead of the entire node

The first case, the need to locate a fragment by string matching, demonstrates the power of XPointer. XPointer uses the same string conformance rules as XPath, which in turn shares rules with XML. Suffice it to say that there are no surprises in the language constraints or conditions because the types of documents are limited to the `text/xml` and other types just listed.

The XPointer expressions use the system of axes, predicates, and functions to locate and select document portions. This is comparable with the tools used by

XPath. XPath works with a data set derived from elements and other constructs of the XML language. XPointer string matching can be applied to the motion picture example XML from previous chapters. For this example, however, let's change the `category` attribute to an element to make the search a little easier:

```xml
<?xml version="1.0"?>
<?xml-stylesheet type="text/xsl" href="filmlibrary.xsl"?>
<filmlibrary>
<motionpicture>
    <title>"The Wizard of Oz"</title>
            <year>1939</year>
        <genre>
            <category>
                musical
            </category>
        </genre>
</motionpicture>
<motionpicture>
    <title>"Duck Soup"</title>
        <year>1933</year>
        <genre>
            <category>
                comedy
            </category>
        </genre>
</motionpicture>
<motionpicture>
    <title>"Gone With the Wind"</title>
        <year>1939</year>
        <genre>
            <category>
                drama
            </category>
        </genre>
</motionpicture>
    .
    .
    .
</filmlibrary>
```

First, a target string is set. In this example, the substring `drama` is searched for, which is found in the `genre` and `category` elements. This allows you to identify any films that are considered dramas and ignore the others. To use this feature, the function `string-range()` is called. This is a basic function that allows simple string matching using a syntax reminiscent of most XML functions. The `string-range()` function takes a node set to search and the desired substring as arguments, returning a range of node sets that contain the substring; therefore, the following says to start at the document root (/) and return node sets containing the substring drama:

```
xpointer(string-range(/, "drama"))
```

Recall the characters (axes) used in expressions to define node context (and node sets): / is root node, // is descendant (or self) node, . is self node, and .. is parent node.

If the substring was sought in a node such as genre, the syntax would be as follows:

```
xpointer(string-range(//genre, "drama"))
```

This also would return node sets in the children of genre (in this case, category). To limit the search to the node sets in *just* genre, the statement would be changed to the following:

```
xpointer(string-range(.genre, "Drama"))
```

Applying this function to the search for a particular year most likely would be started at root so that the title, genre, and so on, as well as the year, will be returned. Therefore, the following returns two node sets as a result—the set containing "The Wizard of Oz" and the set containing "Gone With the Wind"—because both of them have 1939 in the year element:

```
xpointer(string-range(/, "1939"))
```

The string-range() function also can return subsets of the result set. The position of the node in the result set can be specified by position()=n. To return the first occurrence of the year "1939" in the document (starting at /), the function(s) would be expressed as follows:

```
xpointer(string-range(/, "1939")[position()=1])
```

The position() argument would be changed to reflect the second, fourth, or *n*th occurrence of "1939". Other arguments borrowed from XPath for string-range() are as follows:

- The ability to match a portion of a substring
- Positions of the node set in relation to the substring
- The number of characters returned from the substring

XPointer also adds these functions, often used in combinations:

- range() and range-to()
- here() and origin()
- start-point() and end-point()

The range() and range-to() functions provide XPointer with the ability to specify the range to be searched. It accepts a location set as an argument and returns a location set as a result. It will return a location set for each set provided as input. The range() function allows you to specify a range within the document as opposed to a point, which is specified by `position()` in `string-range()`.

A range is defined as any area of the document defined by a `start-point()` and `end-point()`. These points can be referenced by node set or point in the document. If the `start-point()` is set to a location path, multiple location sets are returned as a result. If the `start-point()` is a point, a single set usually should be returned.

The functions `here()` and `origin()` are used to return the element located at the points where the XPointer is located (the `here()` function) or where the traversal began (the `origin()` function).

The `start-point()` and `end-point()` functions are fairly straightforward. The `start-point()` function indicates where the document traversal should begin based on the location-set argument passed into it, returning a location set containing the start points of all the locations found in the input location set. The `end-point()` function provides the end points, used in the same way with the same argument structure. Both start and end points must be in the same document; they cannot span more than one document. Here are some key definitions to keep in mind:

- A location is any node type permitted in XPath.
- A location set is a list of locations.
- A point is a location in an XML document that can be defined as being of a single character in length.
- A range is made up of two points (start and end) and everything in between (markup and all).

XPointer functions often are combined (as the functions in XPath would be) to specify a range. For example, in our XML document earlier, to select the range located between the `motionpicture` and `genre` elements, the XPointer keyword `to` is used. This allows the range to be defined as follows:

```
xpointer(/motionpicture to /genre)
```

This returns the location set of all the nodes between these start and end points, including `genre`.

Another example of a function is

```
here():
      xpointer(here(/ancestor::year/preceding::category
      [2]))
```

This selects as the location the `year` element preceding the second-occurring `category` element. The W3C documentation mentions that the type of the node that uses the `here` function is likely to be text, attributes, or processing instructions. Additionally, the returned location for an XPointer appearing in element content does not have a node type of element because the XPointer is in a text node that is itself inside an element.

8.3   Basic XLinks

XLink expands on the familiar practice of hyperlinks found in (X)HTML and XML. Before exploring XLink (and its application to XML), a bit of review of (X)HTML linking is in order. Recall that (X)HTML hyperlinks have the following characteristics:

- They are one-directional; a document can be linked only one way from one to the other.
- Links are embedded into the (X)HTML; they are part of the document.
- Links may target a portion of the (X)HTML document, but the full document is accessed, not just the requested fragment.
- (X)HTML links can only refer to two resources. The first one is the calling document (the one that contains the hyperlink), and the other is the target document.

With the expanded possibilities of XLink, each of the limitations just noted can be resolved as follows:

- Multiple traversal directions can be specified between resources, avoiding the one-way constraint.
- A hyperlink can be specified as part of an external document, in the same fashion as XSL.
- Using XPointer along with XLink allows a fragment of the document to be linked as a subset of the entire document.
- Links can be defined that include multiple resources, not just the two that (X)HTML can reference.

XLink contains several attributes that supplement the traditional (X)HTML hyperlink:

- The attribute `href` is (still) used in XLink.
- The `type` attribute can be expressed, specifying the type of XLink being created.
- The `role` attribute specifies the resource (in an extended link) in a machine-readable format.
- The `title` attribute specifies the resource (in an extended link) in a human-readable format.
- The `show` attribute specifies the fashion in which the resource shall be displayed.

Starting with `href`, in XLink this attribute is referred to as a *locator attribute,* which means pretty much what it says: It locates a resource based on the URI. The new twist with `href` in XLink is that multiple locator attributes can be declared, as opposed to the single resource available in (X)HTML.

The syntax for the `href` attribute follows the a syntax found in (X)HTML; as shown in the following example:

(X)HTML: `<a href="http://www.someplace.com/">descriptive text</a>`

XLink: `<anyelement xlink:href="http://www.someplace.com/">descriptive text</anyelement>`

The `type` attribute adds the capability of defining the link type, which is mandatory in links:

- `simple`. Defines an entire link, a common link.
- `extended`. Defines an entire link, including outbound and third-party links.
- `locator`. Indicates remote resources (by URI).
- `arc`. Establishes rules for traversing within the linked document.
- `resource`. Defines the different resource types composing the link.
- `title`. Defines a human-readable label for the link.

There is a very informative table of these attributes and their relationships to the other attributes located at `www.w3.org/TR/xlink/#N1238`. We reproduce that table as Table 8-1 for your convenience (see W3C copyright information at `www.w3.org/Consortium/Legal/ipr-notice-20000612#Copyright`). In this table, each element type has an indicator of whether an attribute is required (R) or optional (O).

Table 8-1　Attributes and Their Relationships to Other Attributes

	Simple	Extended	Locator	Arc	Resource	Title
type	R	R	R	R	R	R
href	O		R			
role	O	O	O		O	
arcrole	O			O		
title	O	O	O	O	O	
show	O			O		
actuate	O			O		
label			O		O	
from				O		
to				O		

Using this table as a guide, it is apparent that for element type `simple`, the `type` attribute is required, but the rest are optional. Additionally, it should be obvious that the `type` attribute is required for all element types.

Next, the `role` attribute is designed to provide a machine-readable attribute. This is specific to the needs of XML because XML is meant to be shared between software applications as well as to be human-readable. Because XML is meant to be shared, the `title` attribute is made available for human-readability and for identification of an element.

Finally, XLink defines the `show` attribute, which is similar to `target` in (X)HTML. This provides for opening a new window—similar `target="_blank"` in (X)HTML—or `replace`—comparable with `target="_self"`. XLink also has `embed`, which indicates that a resource should replace an element—as `img` does in (X)HTML—or `undefined`, which allows the link to be displayed based on UA definitions (such as sound media or other MIME content). Helper applications may be required to show the element, but this is left to the discretion of the user.

8.4   Extended XLinks

XLink adds new functionality and dimensionality to the standard, familiar link of (X)HTML. Extended XLink provides the mechanism for connecting an arbitrary number of resources. You can create very complex link structures with both inbound links (as well as standard one-way links) making up the aggregate collection of resources. Some extended XLinks can point to local resources, remote resources, or a combination of both.

Extended XLinks can provide a separate resource to define the links, allowing the storage of extended linking elements to be maintained independent of the primary document. By linking in this fashion, an XLink element might be able to provide a wide range of resources in a format that is as simple to create and maintain as a style sheet.

Another way to view the extended XLink model is that the extended link serves as a hub for related resource links. For example, in the `motionpicture.xml` example, extended links could be created for the `actor` element by providing links for other films by that actor or other links for that actor such as links to a biography.

Extended links provide the commonality, or glue, that connects the resources. This is accomplished by associating an arbitrary number of resources, remote or local. An extended link is the only type of link that is capable of inbound and third-party arcs. These extended arcs are the only element type that can use the functions `from()` and `to()` to provide direction to the linked resource.

Using the `arc` element, the syntax for an extended XLink, including `from()` and `to()`, is applied to the `title` element:

```
<motionpicture
xlink:href="posters.xml"
```

```
xlink:type="extended">
    <title xlink:type="arc"
        xlink:from="motionpicture:title"
        xlink:to="motionpicture:poster"
xlink:show="replace"
xlink:actuate="onRequest"
xlink:role="motionpicture:GetPosterImage"
xlink:title="Get an Image of the Movie Poster">
        "The Wizard of Oz"
    </title>
</motionpicture>
```

Figure 8-1 shows this in diagram form.

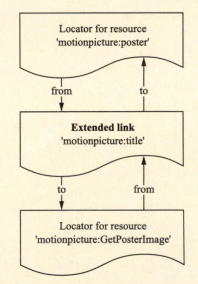

Fig. 8-1.   An XLink document in diagram form.

8.5   Use of XBase

XML Base (XBase) creates the equivalent of the (X)HTML base element in an XML document by providing a URI base for the document *other than* the default base URI of the document or entity. This feature is accessed by the xml:base statement into the document at the preamble stage. If the XML example used previously needed to have a base URI set different from the default, it would be defined as follows:

```
<?xml version="1.0"?>
<doc xml:base="http://alternate.filmstuff.com/"
```

```
    xmlns:xlink="http://www.w3c.org/1999/xlink">
<?xml-stylesheet type="text/xsl" href="filmlibrary.xsl"?>
<filmlibrary>
<motionpicture>
    <title>"The Wizard of Oz"</title>
        <year>1939</year>
        <genre>
            <category>
                musical
            </category>
        </genre>
</motionpicture>
<motionpicture>
    <title>"Duck Soup"</title>
        <year>1933</year>
        <genre>
            <category>
                comedy
            </category>
        </genre>
</motionpicture>
<motionpicture>
    <title>"Gone With the Wind"</title>
        <year>1939</year>
        <genre>
            <category>
                drama
            </category>
        </genre>
</motionpicture>
.
.
.
</filmlibrary>
```

The following statement specifies that the new base URI is found at http://alternate.filmstuff.com and that the linking specification is found at http://www.w3c.org/1999/xlink:

```
<doc xml:base="http://alternate.filmstuff.com/"
xmlns:xlink="http://www.w3c.org/1999/xlink">
```

Any other links (URIs) that share the same XLink namespace and are fully qualified will be followed as stated. This base only affects local links.

Rules established for the resolution of relative URIs are found at www.w3.org/TR/xmlbase/#rfc2396 and are presented here. The rules for determining the base URI can be summarized as follows (highest priority to lowest):

1. The base URI is embedded in the document's content.
2. The base URI is that of the encapsulating entity (message, document, or none).
3. The base URI is the URI used to retrieve the entity.
4. The base URI is defined by the context of the application.

As you can see from this list, there is a cascading effect to URI resolution similar in nature to the CSS hierarchy. One note, though, is that *entity* is used in a slightly different context in the XBase rules just listed. Entity is used in this case per RFC 2396 (Uniform Resource Identifiers) as meaning a unit or string as opposed to the XML sense of entity being a parameter reference. The base URI of an element is (from the W3C XBase Documentation at `www.w3.org/TR/xmlbase/#granularity`)

- The base URI specified by an `xml:base` attribute of the element

or

- The base URI of the element's parent element within the document or external entity

or

- The base URI of the document entity or external entity containing the element

The W3C further specifies four points used to establish a means for matching document URIs with base URIs. These are used to determine a relative URI that appears in an XML document as it is affected or modified by the `xml:base` declaration or the lack of an `xml:base` declaration. The base, according to the W3C, a URI corresponding to any given relative URI appearing in an XML document, is determined as follows:

- The base URI for a URI reference appearing in text content is the base URI of the element containing the text.

- The base URI for a URI reference appearing in an `xml:base` attribute is the base URI of the parent element of the element bearing the `xml:base` attribute if one exists within the document entity or external entity; otherwise, it is the base URI of the document entity or external entity containing the element.

- The base URI for a URI reference appearing in any other attribute value, including default attribute values, is the base URI of the element bearing the attribute.

- The base URI for a URI reference appearing in the content of a processing instruction is the base URI of the parent element of the processing instruction, if one exists, within the document entity or external entity. Otherwise, it is the base URI of the document entity or external entity containing the processing instruction.

(This list is quoted from the W3C at `www.w3.org/TR/xmlbase/#matching`—Section 4.3, "Matching URIs with Base URIs.")

The W3C documentation also provides this note (or warning, perhaps) at `www.w3.org/TR/2000/WD-xmlbase-20000607#IDwkAq1`. The emphasis has been added.

> The presence of `xml:base` attributes might lead to unexpected results in the case where the attribute value is provided, not directly in the XML document entity, but via a default attribute declared in an external entity. Such declarations *might not* be read by software which is based on a non-validating XML processor. Many XML applications fail to require validating processors. For correct operation with such applications, `xml:base` values should be provided either directly or via default attributes declared in the internal subset of the DTD.

Review Questions

8.1 Why does XPointer offer extensions to XPath?

   a. To locate information via string matching
   b. To define points and ranges
   c. To define nodes
   d. To define locations
   e. All of the above

8.2 Does XPointer offer access to the internal structure of the DTD?

8.3 Does XPointer offer access to the internal structure of the schema?

8.4 What media types will XPointer work with?

   a. `text/xml`
   b. `text/html`
   c. `application/xml`
   d. `text/xml-external-parsed-entity`

8.5 Which two of these are functions of XPointer?

   a. `string-range()`
   b. `here()`
   c. `now()`
   d. `parent()`

8.6 Is a point more than one location?

8.7 What is a range?

   a. An area between two points
   b. An area specified by nodes
   c. An area at the beginning of the document
   d. An area between elements

8.8 What is a location?

   a. A node in the document
   b. A node that includes points and ranges
   c. An element made up of points
   d. Part of an axis

8.9 What is a location set?

   a. A collection of points
   b. Points and nodes
   c. A collection of locations
   d. Pairs of points

8.10 What is an arc?

   a. A set of traversal rules
   b. A curve of points
   c. A sequence of locations
   d. The preamble of an XML document

8.11 Name two axis nodes.

8.12 What is a subresource?

   a. The part of the document that is not seen
   b. An alternate bit of content
   c. The portion of the document returned by XPointer
   d. An alternate path through the document

8.13 What conditions are ideal for XPointer?

   a. The need to use string-matching to locate information
   b. The need to append URIs
   c. The need to address a portion of the document
   d. All of the above

8.14 XPointer uses the system of axes, predicates, and functions. True or false?

8.15 Does XPointer use the same location path characters as XPath?

Answers to Review Questions

8.1 e

8.2 No, XPointer is *not* intended or designed to address the internal structure of the DTD of an XML resource, even though it is intended to address fragments of an XML document.

8.3 Yes, a schema is valid XML.

8.4 a, c, and d. Also: `application/xml-external-parsed-entity`.

8.5 a and b

8.6 No, a point is a *place* in the document of a single character length or a single node point.

8.7 a

8.8 b

8.9 c

8.10 a

8.11 Any two of these: child, parent, self, ancestor, ancestor-or-self, attribute, descendant, descendant-or-self, following, following-sibling, namespace, preceding, preceding-sibling

8.12 c

8.13 d

8.14 True. XPointer uses the system of axes, predicates, and functions.

8.15 Yes, XPointer uses the same location path characters as XPath.

CHAPTER 9

XML Security

9.1 Authentication Codes and Digital Signatures

On the Internet in general, and for the Extensible Markup Language (XML) world in particular, there's a strong emphasis on security to ensure the privacy and confidentiality of communications on a public medium, and also to protect the integrity of electronic business transactions. These broad concerns help explain why several working groups at the World Wide Web Consortium (W3C) are currently working on a variety of security initiatives. These include the XML Signature recommendation, which covers use of digital signatures to ensure document integrity, to provide message authentication, and to support signer authentication services. They also include work underway on an XML Encryption initiative; its job is to define strong encryption/decryption services for XML documents, and the XML Key Management working group; its job is to define simple client access to public key data. Outside the W3C, numerous other security-related initiatives for e-commerce, security markup, security assertions, and Web security are also underway. (For an excellent illustration of what's available on this topic, visit `http://www.oasis-open.org/cover/` and search on the term "security".)

As XML becomes more commonplace, the need for security only increases. Such concerns go beyond the encryption used in online purchases through Secure Sockets Layer (SSL) or 128-bit encryption of a customer's credit card data. As the topics of the foregoing W3C recommendations, working groups, and private initiatives attest to, such concerns focus more on the identity or authenticity of the parties that are requesting (or sending) data between XML applications. Thus, typical security concerns, such as AAA (pronounced "triple-A," standing for administration, authorization, and authentication), which deal with how identity is established and managed, what kinds of access or capability proofs of identity confer, and how identity may be proven, are making themselves important in ongoing XML development and activity.

To that end, numerous XML markup languages incorporate or support various systems of digital signatures, extensions and management of confirmation and trust, and various proofs of identity and nonrepudiation of transactions (to prevent individuals from denying that they authorized such transactions later on). The document "XML-Signature Syntax and Processing," a Recommendation approved on February 12, 2002, forms the basis for this chapter. It can be accessed at the W3C Web site at `http://www.w3.org/TR/xmldsig-core/`. The design philosophy for this Recommendation appears in "XML-Signature Requirements," on the W3C Web site at `http://www.w3.org/TR/xmldsig-requirements`.

Just as a point of review, the W3C defined *Canonical XML* as a Working Recommendation on March 15, 2001, stating the following:

> Any XML document is part of a set of XML documents that are logically equivalent within an application context, but which vary in physical representation based on syntactic changes permitted by XML 1.0 and Namespaces in XML. This specification describes a method for generating a physical representation—the canonical form—of an XML document that accounts for the permissible changes. Except for limitations regarding a few unusual cases, if two documents have the same canonical form, then the two documents are logically equivalent within the given application context. Note that two documents may have differing canonical forms yet still be equivalent in a given context based on application-specific equivalence rules for which no generalized XML specification could account.

Some of the key points that appear in this W3C document are

- The specification describes what's involved in signing digital content in general, and XML content in particular. Specific XML markup and syntax that represents a signature affixed to any such XML content is called an *XML-signature*.

- To generate an XML-signature, a special mathematical function called a *hash* is applied to the canonical form of some XML content to create a *signature manifest*. This manifest includes all references to Web resources, the mathematical hash for each resource's content, and may optionally also define each resource's content type.

- The XML-signature syntax permits the content of resources that appears in a signature manifest to be encrypted using an associated key that supports a strong one-way transformation (this is what the hash function is all about).

- XML-signature syntax is designed to be readily extensible. This permits an XML-signature to accommodate various kinds of certificate-based services and certificate checks and trusts; it also permits various kinds of statements about the type of security afforded thereby to be made (called *assertion capabilities*). In fact, designations for such capabilities, checks, and assertions can themselves be incorporated into a signature manifest and can thus themselves be signed.

- The XML-signature specification requires that all key information used to check the validity of the cryptographic signature (for example, the public key member of a public/private key pair) be provided.

- To work properly, an XML-signature specification must supply or point to one or more methods to canonicalize (make the XML content meet requirements for Canonical XML stated earlier) and hash (drive the mathematical function that encrypts the digest contents) the XML content.

- To ensure compatibility with existing XML applications and environments, XML-signature applications must conform to the specifications for XML namespaces, XLink, and X-Pointers.

This base document goes on to state that an XML signature must be an XML element, as defined by the XML specification, and must abide by the root element of the document and not conflict with the document's content model; that is, it must maintain consistency with the dependencies in the XML document tree.

Most of the work related to digital signatures hinges on the premise that such signatures must provide integrity, confidence, and nonreputability. This means that a signature should ensure that message contents cannot be changed, inspected, or later denied by their senders. This is vitally important for financial transactions, payments, contracts, and business items, such as purchase orders and the like. Any document that could be produced on paper, signed, sealed, and delivered, ideally should have an electronic (and in this case, an XML) equivalent. It's not unreasonable to speculate that both Resource Description Framework (RDF) and Platform for Privacy Preferences (P3P) will be major players in the XML security future.

The current XML-signature recommendation defines a *signature element* to contain all information required to process a digital signature. This means that some external proof of a signer's identity (such as a validity confirmation from a certificate authority) is vital, as is the expectation that encryption based on such a signature is strong enough to resist decryption or tampering.

To be valid, a digital signature should incorporate one of the following *signature elements:*

- An XML element that contains the necessary information in-line—that is, inside the signature element itself

- An external XML document where the necessary information resides, indicated by a URI

- Some other external non-XML resource, which must also be identified by a URI

9.2 The Signature Element

The XML digital signature is represented by the `Signature` element (recall that in SGML DTD syntax, ? denotes zero or one occurrence, + denotes one or more occurrences, and * denotes zero or more occurrences). The `Signature` element is

```
<Signature>
    <SignedInfo>
```

```
        (CanonicalizationMethod)?
        (SignatureMethod)
        <Reference URI=? >
            (Transforms)?
            (DigestMethod)
            (DigestValue)
        </Reference>)+
    </SignedInfo>
    (SignatureValue)
    (KeyInfo)?
    (Object)*
</Signature>
```

Now let's dissect this markup line by line:

- The `Signature` element is the root element for an XML-signature. This opens and closes the signature method following standard XML syntax.

- The structure of the `SignedInfo` element includes the canonicalization algorithm (which is optional), a signature algorithm, and zero or more references. It also might include an optional ID attribute so it may be referenced by other elements.

- The `CanonicalizationMethod` specifies the algorithm used on the `SignedInfo` element *prior* to performing signature calculations. The default canonicalization method is called *Canonical XML*.

- `SignatureMethod` is a required element. It specifies the algorithm used for signature generation and validation, for example, public key algorithms, hashing, or message authentication codes (MACs). The encoding methods for all `SignatureMethods` specified in the W3C specification are all base64 (MIME). Also, user-specified algorithms, with their own encodings, are allowed.

- The `Reference` element may occur one or more times. It specifies a digest value and algorithm. It may further specify an identifier for the object being signed and/or a list of transformations to be applied prior to digesting. The identifier and the transforms describe how digested content is created. If the data being signed is an XML document, the document is assumed to be unparsed prior to the application of transforms. If there are no transforms, the data is passed to the digest algorithm unmodified.

- Each transform is made up of an algorithm attribute and content parameters appropriate to the particular algorithm in use. The `Transform` element is optional and contains an ordered list of `Transform` elements that describes how the signer obtained the data object that was digested. The *output* of each `Transform` element serves as *input* to the next `Transform`. The input to the first `Transform` is the source data, and the output from the last `Transform` is the input for the `DigestMethod` algorithm. When transforms are applied, the signer is not signing the original document *but* the resulting, transformed document.

- The `DigestMethod` element is required, and it identifies the digest algorithm to be applied to the signed object.

- The `DigestValue` is the element that contains the encoded value of the digest and is always encoded using base64.

- The `SignatureValue` element contains the actual value of the digital signature, and it is encoded according to the identifier specified in `SignatureMethod`.

- The `KeyInfo` element is optional and enables the recipient to obtain the key (or keys) needed to validate a signature. The `KeyInfo` element may contain keys, names, certificates, and other public key management information, such as key distribution or key agreement data. If `KeyInfo` is left out, one is expected to be able to identify the key based on application context information.

- In the case of envelope signatures, it is the `Object` element that contains the object being signed. The digest is calculated over the entire `Object` element, including its `Object` tags. `Object` is an optional element that may occur one or more times.

Let's look at a sample `Signature` element that contains data. This is from the XML-Signature Candidate Recommendation:

```
<Signature Id="MySignatureExample"
        xmlns="http://www.w3.org/2000/09/xmldsig#">
```

This markup states that the signature has an ID, `MySignatureExample`, and is part of the namespace found at the stated URI. It is closed in the last line of the following example:

```
<SignedInfo>
   <CanonicalizationMethod
       Algorithm="http://www.w3.org/TR/2000/CR-xml-c14n-
       20001026"/>
   <SignatureMethod
       Algorithm="http://www.w3.org/2000/09/xmldsig#dsa-
       sha1"/>
   <Reference URI="http://www.w3.org/TR/2000/REC-xhtml1-
       20000126/">
       <Transforms>
          <Transform
          Algorithm="http://www.w3.org/TR/2000/CR-xml-
          c14n-20001026"/>
       </Transforms>
       <DigestMethod
       Algorithm="http://www.w3.org/2000/09/
       xmldsig#sha1"/>
         <DigestValue>j6lwx3rvEPO0vKtMup4NbeVu8nk=
         </DigestValue>
   </Reference>
</SignedInfo>
```

The preceding markup describes the element in more detail, using some optional attributes. CanonicalizationMethod is described as using the Algorithm found at the stated URI. The Reference and Transform describe how the digested content was created, again found at the stated URIs. The DigestMethod and DigestValue define the Algorithm and the encoded value for the digest. Both are required.

```
<Signature>
...
<SignatureValue>MC0CFFrVLtRlk=...</SignatureValue>
    <KeyInfo>
        <KeyValue>
            <DSAKeyValue>
                <P>...</P><Q>...</Q><G>...</G><Y>...</Y>
            </DSAKeyValue>
        </KeyValue>
    </KeyInfo>
</Signature>
```

This markup shows that the SignatureValue contains the actual value of the digital signature, and is encoded according to the identifier specified in SignatureMethod. These are required elements. There are also the KeyInfo and KeyValue elements and the name of any additional keys in this code. These are optional, depending on the needs of the document and its method of encryption. Compare the preceding example with the Document Type Declaration (DTD) presented earlier to get a sense of what is required and what is optional.

9.3　Canonicalization Choices

It's possible to modify XML documents extensively without changing their meaning. Such changes usually involve text handling, so that changes to indentation, pagination, line spacing, line breaks, and so forth have no real effect on the document's content. This explains why changing such things should not impact hashing calculations, and why conversion of XML documents to canonical form before hashing occurs is so important. Because the canonical form ignores these kinds of differences between versions of otherwise identical documents, it's the foundation on which signature hashing rests. The canonical form of an XML document results from applying the method described in the Canonical XML version 1.0 specification (http://www.w3.org/TR/xml-c14n).

A summary of the terminology from this W3C document appears in the following list, quoted from the preceding specification document:

- The document is encoded in UTF-8.
- Line breaks are normalized to #xA on input, before parsing.
- Attribute values are normalized, as if done by a validating processor.

- Character and parsed entity references are replaced.

- CDATA sections are replaced with their character content.

- The XML declaration and DTD are removed.

- Empty elements are converted to start tag/end tag pairs.

- White space outside the document element (and within start and end tags) is normalized.

- All white space in character content is retained (excluding any characters removed during line feed normalization).

- Attribute value delimiters are set in quotation marks (double quotes).

- Special characters in attribute values and character content are replaced by character references.

- Superfluous namespace declarations are removed from each element.

- Default attributes are added to each element.

The term *Canonical XML* therefore refers to XML that is in canonical form. The *XML canonicalization method* is the algorithm defined by the specification that generates the canonical form of a given XML document or document subset. The term *XML canonicalization* refers to the process of applying the XML canonicalization method to an XML document or document subset.

Remember, the canonical form is necessary to produce a version of an XML document that ignores trivial differences and concentrates entirely on the actual content. When comparing the digest calculated for a version of a document as received to the digest calculated for the version of the document that existed before it was sent, equality provides a reasonable guarantee that no tampering occurred in transit, and inequality provides positive proof that some alterations did indeed occur.

9.4 Digest and Signature Choices

When a digital signature is calculated, a software program must create a digest of the document or content being signed. Numerous algorithms for creating digests are available, so whichever algorithm is used to create a digest must be identified in the `Signature` element for validation following its delivery to a recipient. Essentially, this algorithm performs a mathematical operation called a hash on the document's content to produce a single large numeric value known as a digest. The algorithm is sensitive enough to the most minor changes in content so that even a slight change (the alteration of a single character will do) produces a markedly different digest value. By delivering the digest along with the content, and then recomputing that digest value later, comparison will indicate if the document is the same (and has the same digest value) or has been altered (and has a different digest value).

To protect the contents of a digital signature, it's also customary to encrypt the digest using the signer's private key (as covered in the `KeyValue` and `KeyInfo` elements). Upon receipt, the signer's public key is used to decrypt the signature and unlock the original digest. Afterwards, a recalculation of the hash and a comparison between the digest as calculated and as sent will conclusively indicate if a message is unaltered or otherwise. The value of encryption is that it provides positive proof of the signer's identity (only someone who holds the signer's private key can produce text that the signer's public key decrypts) at that same time that it verifies the integrity of the document's contents. These operations occur in the background, and are unnoticeable to users unless errors or tampering is detected.

9.5   The KeyInfo Element

The `KeyInfo` element is completely described in the W3C recommendation ("XML-Signature Syntax and Processing," W3C Recommendation, February 12, 2002) but may be summarized as follows. Essentially, this element specifies the key to be used to validate a signature, where identifiers might include digital certificates, key names, or key agreement algorithms and related information. As it happens, `KeyInfo` is optional for one of two reasons: first, a signer may not wish to explicitly disclose key information to all parties who receive a document (and perhaps rely on an already shared secret key), and second, a receiving application may already have access to such information and not need it to be disclosed. The `KeyInfo` element occurs outside the `SignedInfo` element, so a `Reference` can be used to associate keying information to a signature, as well as to identify and include specific `Keyinfo` elements.

The following is a sample of correct syntax for the `KeyInfo` element:

```
<KeyInfo>
<KeyValue>
<DSAKeyValue>
<P>...</P><Q>...</Q><G>...</G><Y>...</Y>
</DSAKeyValue>
</KeyValue>
</KeyInfo>
```

This markup states that the `KeyInfo` element is one that (as an option) allows the recipient, or recipients, of a document to locate and obtain whatever key is needed to validate a document signature. A key itself may contain keys, names, certificates, and other public key management information, such as key agreement data. If the `KeyInfo` element is omitted, the recipient is expected to be able to identify the key based on application context. Multiple declarations contained within the `KeyInfo` element all refer to the *same* key. If the `KeyInfo` element appears, it often contains the elements `KeyName`, `KeyValue`, or other PCDATA values that specify necessary `KeyInfo` values. The most commonly used such element is `KeyName`, which identifies a string that the signer can use to communicate a key identifier to the recipient. `KeyName` typically contains an identifier related to the key pair used to sign the message, but may contain other information to identify a key pair indirectly. It is typical for `KeyName` to include simple string names for keys, a key index, or an e-mail address to identify a key pair.

The `KeyValue` element contains a single public key that may be used to validate a signature. Structured formats to define Directory System Agent (DSA) and Rivest, Shamir, and Adleman (RSA) public keys appear in the Signature Algorithms section of the XML-Signature syntax and processing specification. A `KeyValue` element may include externally defined public key values represented as PCDATA or element types from an external namespace.

The schemas (and DTDs) for all the `KeyInfo` components are

KeyName:

SCHEMA:

```
<element name="KeyName" type="string"/>
```

DTD:

```
<!ELEMENT KeyName (#PCDATA) >
```

KeyValue:

SCHEMA:

```
<element name="KeyValue" type="ds:KeyValueType"/>
<complexType name="KeyValueType" mixed="true">
<choice>
<element ref="ds:DSAKeyValue"/>
<element ref="ds:RSAKeyValue"/>
<any namespace="##other" processContents="lax"/>
</choice>
</complexType>
```

DTD:

```
<!ELEMENT KeyValue (#PCDATA|DSAKeyValue|RSAKeyValue
    %KeyValue.ANY;)* >
```

`DSAKeyValue` fields `P`, `Q`, `G`, and `Y` are mandatory; other value fields, `J`, `seed`, and `pgenCounter`, are optional, but should be included when this kind of key value is used.

SCHEMA:

```
<element name="DSAKeyValue" type="ds:DSAKeyValueType"/>
<complexType name="DSAKeyValueType">
<sequence>
<sequence>
<element name="P" type="ds:CryptoBinary"/>
<element name="Q" type="ds:CryptoBinary"/>
<element name="G" type="ds:CryptoBinary"/>
<element name="Y" type="ds:CryptoBinary"/>
<element name="J" type="ds:CryptoBinary" minOccurs="0"/>
```

```
</sequence>
<sequence minOccurs="0">
<element name="Seed" type="ds:CryptoBinary"/>
<element name="PgenCounter" type="ds:CryptoBinary"/>
</sequence>
</sequence>
</complexType>
```

DTD:

```
<!ELEMENT DSAKeyValue (P, Q, G, Y, J?, (Seed, PgenCounter)?) >
<!ELEMENT P (#PCDATA) >
<!ELEMENT Q (#PCDATA) >
<!ELEMENT G (#PCDATA) >
<!ELEMENT Y (#PCDATA) >
<!ELEMENT J (#PCDATA) >
<!ELEMENT Seed (#PCDATA) >
<!ELEMENT PgenCounter (#PCDATA) >
```

The RSAKeyValue element has two fields: Modulus and Exponent:

SCHEMA:

```
<element name="RSAKeyValue" type="ds:RSAKeyValueType"/>
<complexType name="RSAKeyValueType">
<sequence>
<element name="Modulus" type="ds:CryptoBinary"/>
<element name="Exponent" type="ds:CryptoBinary"/>
</sequence>
</complexType>
```

DTD:

```
<!ELEMENT RSAKeyValue (Modulus, Exponent) >
<!ELEMENT Modulus (#PCDATA) >
<!ELEMENT Exponent (#PCDATA) >
```

Use the RetrievalMethod element within KeyInfo to convey a reference to
KeyInfo information stored at some other location (rather than in the current
XML document itself).

SCHEMA:

```
<element name="RetrievalMethod"
        type="ds:RetrievalMethodType"/>
<complexType name="RetrievalMethodType">
<sequence>
<element name="Transforms" type="ds:TransformsType"
        minOccurs="0"/>
</sequence>
<attribute name="URI" type="anyURI"/>
<attribute name="Type" type="anyURI" use="optional"/>
```

```
</complexType>
```

DTD:

```
<!ELEMENT RetrievalMethod (Transforms?) >
<!ATTLIST RetrievalMethod URI CDATA #REQUIRED Type CDATA
      #IMPLIED >
```

9.6   Transformations and Use of XPath

It may be necessary to apply transformations elements to the `Signature`. These elements are children of the `Reference` element and include the `Transforms` and `Transform Algorithm` elements.

The W3C describes `Transforms` as

> . . . an optional ordered list of processing steps that were applied to the resource's content before it was digested. Transforms can include operations such as canonicalization, encoding/decoding (including compression/inflation), XSLT and XPath. XPath transforms permit the signer to derive an XML document that omits portions of the source document. Consequently those excluded portions can change without affecting signature validity. For example, if the resource being signed encloses the signature itself, such a transform must be used to exclude the signature value from its own computation. If no transforms element is present, the resource's content is digested directly. While we specify mandatory (and optional) canonicalization and decoding algorithms, user specified transforms are permitted.

The series of processing steps that define a transform is the recipe to follow, where XPath provides a means to find the necessary ingredients to which the recipe applies. If we examine a typical `Transforms` element, we will see how its different components interlock, and how it applies to XML-Signatures.

To aid your understanding, here are some quick definitions of terms relevant to transforms:

- *XPath*. The XML Path Language (XPath) is a W3C standard declarative language used to traverse the Document Object Model (DOM) based on that model's tree-node structure. XPath defines a way to identify and access portions or subsets of XML documents. XPath uses a path-based syntax that is similar to syntaxes used in file systems or for document retrieval. XPath covers addressing needs relevant to XPointer (see Chapter 8) and pattern matching used in the Extensible Stylesheet Language Transformations (XSLT, covered in Chapter 7). XPath provides a common foundation to solve a fundamental problem in XML: that is, the need to locate elements, attributes, and other XML document content using concise and convenient notation. (See Chapter 6 for a full treatment.)

- *Hashing.* This is an algorithm that generates a unique numeric value based on the content of transaction data so that it can be verified by recipients using the same algorithm by comparing the value as sent to the value as calculated upon receipt (called a checksum) to ensure that content is unaltered.

- *Encryption and decryption.* Information may be sent in an illegible (encrypted) form between two (or more) parties. On receipt, it can be decrypted using the appropriate key and returned to a legible form. This is done by using an algorithm, such as hashing.

In practice, the process is as follows:

1. Every transform is made up of an `algorithm` attribute and holds any content parameters appropriate to the algorithm used. The `algorithm` attribute specifies the name of the algorithm to be applied, and the transform content provides any additional data for the algorithm's processing of the transform.

2. As described in the W3C's"The Reference Processing Model," some transforms take an XPath node set as input, whereas others require an octet stream.

3. If the actual input matches the input requirements of the transform, then the transform operates on the unaltered input.

4. If the transform input requirement differs from the format of the actual input, then the input must be converted.

5. If transforms require an explicit MIME type, charset, or other such information that concerns the data they are receiving from an earlier transform or the source data, the data characteristics are provided as parameters to the transform algorithm and are described in the specification for the algorithm itself.

Let's look at a DTD for `Transforms`, a schema, and then an example; first, the DTD:

```
<!ELEMENT Transforms (Transform+)>
<!ELEMENT Transform (#PCDATA|XPath %Transform.ANY;)* >
    <!ATTLIST Transform Algorithm CDATA #REQUIRED >
<!ELEMENT XPath (#PCDATA) >
```

This defines the `Transforms` element as being made up of one or more `Transform` elements, which in turn consists of either #PCDATA (parsed character data) or an XPath statement and the parameter entity `%Transform.ANY`, which permits users to include their own element types. This may appear zero or more times. The `Transform` element has the required attributes of `Algorithm` and CDATA. Finally, the element `XPath` is included as #PCDATA.

The schema is

```
<element name="Transforms" type="ds:TransformsType"/>
    <complexType name="TransformsType">
        <sequence>
```

```
        <element ref="ds:Transform"
        maxOccurs="unbounded"/>
    </sequence>
  </complexType>
  <element name="Transform" type="ds:TransformType"/>
  <complexType name="TransformType" mixed="true">
      <choice minOccurs="0" maxOccurs="unbounded">
          <any namespace="##other"
          processContents="lax"/>
          <!-- (1,1) elements from (0,unbounded)
          namespaces -->
          <element name="XPath" type="string"/>
      </choice>
      <attribute name="Algorithm" type="anyURI"
      use="required"/>
  </complexType>
```

The schema presents the same overall definition, starting with `Transforms` and all the subelements and the attribute `Algorithm`. For example:

```
<?xml version="1.0"?>
<!DOCTYPE Signature (View Source for full doctype...)>
<Signature Id="MyFirstSignature"
xmlns="http://www.w3.org/2000/09/xmldsig#"
xmlns:xsi="http://www.w3.org/2001/XMLSchema-instance"
        xsi:schemaLocation="http://www.w3.org/2000/09/
        xmldsig#xmldsig-core-schema.xsd">
<SignedInfo>
<CanonicalizationMethod
        Algorithm="http://www.w3.org/TR/2000/WD-xml-c14n-
        20000710" />
<SignatureMethod
        Algorithm="http://www.w3.org/2000/09/xmldsig#dsa"
        />
<Reference URI="http://www.w3.org/TR/xml-stylesheet/">
<Transforms>
<Transform
        Algorithm="http://www.w3.org/2000/09/
        xmldsig#base64"/>
<Transform
        Algorithm="http://www.w3.org/2000/09/xmldsig#null"
        />
</Transforms>
...
</Signature>
```

After the initial processing instruction (PI) and DOCTYPE declaration, we find the element `Signature`, with namespace and schema location defined. Next, we find the `SignatureMethod` and `Reference` elements, and finally the `Transforms` element. In this example, we use two `Transform` elements, each of which declares an algorithm (as an XPath).

9.7 Encryption

XML encryption revolves around the `EncryptedNode` element. This is the central player and sets the stage for what follows. It has an attribute `NodeType` that indicates the type of node that has been encrypted. This might be element, element content, attribute, or an attributes value. The `EncryptedNode` itself is a base64-encoded string that forms the content of the element.

Algorithm and keying information are held in the `EncryptionInfo` element. Each `EncryptedNode` element has an `EncryptionInfo` element. The association between them may be accomplished either by having the element as the first child element of the `EncryptedNode` element *or* by pointing to the element through the `EncryptionInfo` attribute of the element. Applications create the `EncryptionInfo` element to store the information necessary for decryption. Multiple `EncryptedNode` elements may share a single `EncryptionInfo` element.

Additionally, XML encryption supports the ability to store (one or more) objects in encrypted form. These objects can be content such as text, CSS, a JPEG image, or any other type of arbitrary object, including the entire XML document. To accomplish this, the `EncryptedNode` element possesses two child elements:

- The `EncryptedNodes` element for holding one or more `EncryptedNode` elements
- The `EncryptedInfos` element for holding one or more `EncryptedInfo` elements

Each `EncryptedNode` element contains the encrypted data for *one* object. Keep in mind that an `Encryption` element may contain only an `EncryptedNodes` element *or* only an `EncryptedInfos` element but not both.

A special value or number called a key is used to keep encrypted information secret. When combined with a specific algorithm, such a key can produce an encrypted result for transmission, or it (or a companion member of a pair of keys) can decrypt information upon transmission. Because the algorithm itself might be widely known, the key is the necessary secret component needed to keep information confidential and secure. If a key is complex enough, encryption remains secure in the face of even the most determined attacks, and the data is impossible to intercept in a reasonable amount of time.

With symmetric key encryption, an encryption key can be calculated from a decryption key, and vice versa. Public key encryption (also known as *asymmetric encryption*) employs a pair of keys (one public, available to anyone and everyone, the other private, available exclusively to a single user or identity) to establish a digital notion of identity that is strong and reliable. Private/public key pairs enable any user who needs to authenticate his or her identity online to do so, as well as to sign and encrypt data. Examples of asymmetric encryption include RSA, Pretty Good Privacy (PGP), Directory System Agent (DSA), and the SSL (Secure Sockets Layer) protocol.

9.7.1 RSA. RSA PUBLIC KEY ENCRYPTION

In 1978 in a paper entitled, "A Method for Obtaining Digital Signatures and Public Key Cryptosystems," MIT Professors Ronald Rivest and Adi Shamir and USC Professor Leonard Adleman proposed a particular implementation of the Diffie-Hellman concept. Their scheme is now known as the *RSA Public Key Cryptosystem,* after the authors' initials. RSA public key encryption is an asymmetric encryption algorithm. An RSA key has to be generated so that the data can be encrypted. RSA keys have both a public and a private key component. The private key must be kept secret, but the public key may be distributed. If the data is encrypted with the public key, then it must be decrypted with the private key, and if it is encrypted with the private key, it must be decrypted with the public key.

This offers two modes of operation:

- *Encryption*. This uses the public key to encrypt the data and the private key to decrypt it. Thus anyone can encrypt data, but only the private key owner can decrypt it.
- *Signing*. This uses the private key to encrypt the data and the public key to decrypt it. The public key decryption therefore is used as a verification tool to verify that the private key was used for encryption. If the public key decryption succeeds, then this is considered proof that the person encrypting the data had access to an electronic signature in the form of a private key.

Like other asymmetric key algorithms, RSA is orders of magnitude slower than symmetric key algorithms. That's because key sizes are commonly on the order of 512, 768, 1,024 or even longer strings of bits, and involve massive processing to perform necessary calculations for encryption and decryption. Speaking practically, this makes it too expensive to encrypt large amounts of data using asymmetric key algorithms. That's why asymmetric algorithms are used primarily for digital signatures or digests, and to provide a secure method to exchange (much smaller and more efficient) one-time symmetric keys to encrypt session or application traffic between a sender and a receiver. Here are the steps for encryption:

1. A random session key is generated.
2. The payload is encrypted with the session key using a symmetric method.
3. The session key is RSA-encrypted with the public RSA key.
4. The encrypted payload and the encrypted session key are transmitted to the recipient.

The following steps detail the signing process:

1. Checksum/secure tools are used to create a secure checksum of the data.
2. The checksum is RSA-encrypted with the private RSA key.
3. The data and the encrypted are transmitted checksum to the recipient.

9.7.2 DSA

The Digital Signature Algorithm (DSA) was developed by the National Security Agency (NSA) and adopted as a federal information-processing standard (FIPS). The purpose of DSA is to provide a means to electronically sign a document. It is very similar to RSA in overall functionality, but it is used only for signing a document, not for encrypting the document. As is the case with RSA, DSA uses public and private keys. The public key is distributed to allow signature verification, and the private portion is kept secret. DSA is limited by the size of the DSA key—if there are large amounts of data, DSA need to be signed. DSA usually is used in combination with other secure checksum methods.

9.7.3 DH

Whitfield Diffie and Martin Hellman developed the first public key algorithm in 1976. Their algorithm, known as the Diffie Hellman (DH) Key Exchange algorithm may be used to create a session key to encrypt communications between a pair of computers using an insecure line. The recipe for the DH algorithm is:

1. Each party agrees on a large prime number, n, and another number g, so that g modulo n is also a prime number.
2. One party provides a large random integer x and sends the other party the value of g raised to the x power modulo n.
3. The other party provides another large random integer y and sends the first party the value of g raised to the y power modulo n.
4. The first party calculates the value k, equal to y raised to the x power modulo n, and the second party calculates the value k' (pronounced "k-prime") equal to x to the y power modulo n. Mathematics decrees that k and k' produce the same value, namely g raised to the xy power modulo n. Only sender and receiver share the knowledge of k and k', even though all other values may be known.
5. The shared value of k defines a temporary key that serves admirably for symmetric key encryption.

Over time, numerous attacks on DH have proved successful; today, best practice is to pick very large primes (resulting in equally large session keys). Because of the size of the keys involved, RSA algorithms (which seldom exceed 2,048 bits in common practice) may be shorter and therefore faster. In this instance, one party picks a random session key and encrypts it using the recipient's public key; upon receipt the other party uses its private key to decrypt the session key so both parties can begin using it immediately.

9.7.4 IDEA

James L. Massey and Xuejia Lia developed the International Data Encryption Algorithm (IDEA) in Zurich, Switzerland. It was published in its current form (after being modified twice to defeat demonstrated weaknesses) in 1992. IDEA is a block cipher that operates on 64-bit blocks of encrypted text (known as plaintext in cryptographic terms) using a key that is 128 bits long. IDEA also uses the same algorithm to encrypt and decrypt data streams. Although its principles are well known and well understood, IDEA remains resistant to attack and is thought quite strong by most cryptographers. That probably explains why the popular program Pretty Good Privacy (PGP) uses IDEA to encrypt files and electronic mail.

9.7.5 PGP

PGP version 7 uses a variety of encryption algorithms, including IDEA for private key encryption, RSA for public key encryption, as well as DSA, MD5 (Message Digest version 5), and SHA-1 (Secure Hashing Algorithm version 1) to handle encryption, authentication, message integrity, and key management. PGP also handles and verifies digital signatures and includes key management capabilities. PGP stores collections of public and private keys in special files that the program calls *key rings*.

In many instances standard encryption protocols such as SSL are secure enough to provide workable confidentiality for data transmitted across the Internet, but they pick up and deliver all data in plain text form. PGP can encrypt data when it is not in transit—that is, before a message is sent, or when it resides in a file on a local machine after transmission. Such wholesale encryption methods disguise entire XML, not portions of those documents, as with the XML-Signature digest method. When circumstances decree that only certain parts of an XML document need encryption, and the remainder need not be encrypted, more granular methods of encryption may be warranted. Such methods are sometimes called element-wise encryption; they have become a W3C standard as part of the XML digital signature standard described earlier in this chapter.

The W3C recommendation for the XML digital signature standard identifies a set of algorithms to be used in the different `Signature` elements. An important point is that this standard is extensible, and future developers may use alternative algorithms. The algorithms are identified by URIs contained as attribute values in the element that includes the algorithm. Next, we describe briefly some of these specified algorithms and where they are used.

Only one digest algorithm is defined by the W3C, even though newer, stronger ones are expected to be developed in connection with the U.S. Advanced

Encryption Standard effort. The only one defined is SHA-1, and it is used to compute a condensed representation of a message or data file (that is, a digest).

SHA-1 is thought to be secure because it is nearly impossible to find a message that corresponds to a given message digest or to find two different messages that produce the same digest. Any change of any kind to a message during transit results in a different digest, and therefore, the signature fails. The digest algorithm is identified in the `DigestMethod` element.

The message authentication code (MAC) specified by W3C is called *keyed-hashing for message authentication* (HMAC), and it is a means of message authentication using a hashing method. It takes two implicit parameters, the keying material determined from `KeyInfo` and the output stream from the `CanonicalizationMethod`, and it implies a secret key cryptography. The Minimal Canoncalization algorithm is very elementary:

- The character encoding is converted to UTF-8, which is an ASCII-preserving encoding method of Unicode.

- Line endings are normalized as provided by XML using standard characters.

Canonical XML is no more than a strict syntax of XML. Documents may be transformed into Canonical XML, and the result of this transformation is described as the canonical form of the original document. Bear in mind that there is potentially some information loss.

The `Transform` algorithm has a single implicit parameter, which is the octet stream from the `Reference` or the output of an earlier `Transform`. Several `Transform` algorithms are mentioned by W3C, including the `Canonicalization` algorithms mentioned previously. These `Transform` algorithms have different purposes and may look very different depending on what the goal of the transform is.

Here is a set of requirements needed to encrypt an XML document. These are paraphrased from the W3C documents.

- *Element-wise confidentiality*. This allows a portion (that is, a single element) to be encrypted. ". . . Any element in an XML document shall be able to be encrypted. The element may contain subelements, texts, and so on. The rest of the document should remain in plain text. . . ."

- *Well-formedness of an encrypted document*. This states that an encrypted XML document still must follow the rules for well-formedness, just as an unencrypted document does. ". . . the document that is obtained as a result of encrypting some of its element(s) must still be a well-formed XML document. Thus, encryption can be nested. . . ."

- *Information set preservation*. The decrypted and encrypted versions must possess the same information set items. Items cannot be added or deleted by the encryption-decryption process. ". . . Decrypting an encrypted document must provide exactly the same set of core information items as the original document. . . ."

- *Independence from encryption algorithm*. The syntax of encrypted elements should not be dependent on the encryption algorithm. Furthermore, support must be available for both symmetric and asymmetric key encryption schemes.

- *Flexibility of key delivery mechanism.* The encrypted elements' syntax should be flexible with regard to the key exchange method.

- *Independence from outer context.* An encrypted element should be able to be decrypted without having to rely on any outer context. The encrypted element should not be affected by changes to the outer context, that is, character encoding, DOCTYPE, and the like.

- *Compression.* An element should be allowed to be compressed before encryption.

The encryption of an XML document generally follows these steps:

1. A secret key, under which the XML document will be encrypted, is generated. This secret key will be either randomly generated or derived from a pass phrase.

2. The XML document is encoded as a stream of bytes. For example, it simply might be encoded in textual form and translated from that to a stream of bytes.

3. The stream of bytes is encrypted with a symmetric encryption algorithm using the secret key generated earlier.

4. The resulting cipher text is transformed to a textual encoding.

5. If the document is intended for transmission to a particular individual, the secret key is encrypted using that individual's public key, transformed to a textual encoding, and encoded in an XML node.

6. Finally, ancillary information (such as the encryption algorithm used, and so on) is encoded as further XML nodes. The resulting XML nodes are organized into a DTD-defined XML structure and returned to the caller.

For each item to be decrypted,

- The XML document is parsed, and the parameters, key, and algorithm are established.

- The data to be decrypted is determined.

- The data encryption key is also decrypted, if need be, or retrieved from a local resource.

- The data decryption procedure is accomplished.

- If the encrypted data is in an EncryptedData structure and the type is Element or NodeList, the plain-text document must be transformed from UTF-8 into a serialized XML fragment. If this fragment is not well-formed XML, it is converted into the character encoding of the document and replaces the data beginning with the left angle bracket of the start tag of the EncryptedData element and ending with the right angle bracket of the end tag of the EncryptedData element.

In summary, since this area of research and development is evolving almost hourly, we *highly* recommend that you take full advantage of the resources, recommendations, and updates found on the W3C Web site.

Review Questions

9.1 Why is XML security becoming important?

    a. Most electronic business transactions are done via the Web.

    b. HTML has an uncertain future.

    c. Data needs to be authenticated.

    d. All of the above.

9.2 Why is Canonical XML important for digital signatures?

    a. So that the documents mean the same thing

    b. To equalize any differences in the document's meaning

    c. To make the calculation of hashes possible

    d. To be consistent

9.3 Which one of these three things in the `Signature` element is referred to by the signature?

    a. An XML element contained inside the signature element

    b. An external XML document, referenced by a URI

    c. An external non-XML resource, referenced by a URI

    d. Any of them

9.4 What is an advantage to a *public* key system?

    a. The user of the system does not have to be known to you, the owner of the decryption key, in advance. In particular, you do not need a secure means of delivering the encryption key to a user, for knowing only the encryption key does not, in practice, compromise the security of the encryption-decryption system.

    b. The system is difficult to break.

    c. The system is easy to use.

    d. All of the above.

9.5 Which of these is an *asymmetric* encryption method?

    a. Diffie Hellman Key Exchange

    b. DES

    c. RSA

    d. NRA

9.6 In the element `DSAKeyValue`, which of these fields are optional?

    a. `P, G`

    b. `Seed, PgenCounter`

    c. `Q, Y`

    d. None of these

9.7 Which of these are declared in the element `RSAKeyValue`?

      a. Modulus, Exponent
      b. Exponent, KeyValue
      c. Modulus, Remainder
      d. Exponent, Mantissa

9.8 What is hashing?
      a. An element that generates a unique checksum
      b. An algorithm that generates a shared value
      c. An algorithm that generates a unique checksum
      d. An attribute that generates a unique value

9.9 Which of these are common encryption schemes?
      a. RSA Public Key
      b. DSA Digital Signature
      c. PGP
      d. All of these

9.10 Which of these is the strongest encryption?
      a. IDEA
      b. SHA-1
      c. DES
      d. RSA

Answers to Review Questions

9.1 a
9.2 c
9.3 d
9.4 d
9.5 c
9.6 b
9.7 a
9.8 c
9.9 d
9.10 a

Glossary

absolute location path   In XPath, the path for the location that starts at the document root.

action   The portion of a construction rule that describes how a document element (pattern) should be formatted.

API (application programming interface)   A specific collection of programming instructions that allows one program to invoke the functions of a second program (generally an application requesting services from the operating system).

ASCII (American Standard Code for Information Interchange)   A method of coding characters for translation. Characters can include numbers, text, and symbols, which are rendered into digital form. ASCII includes only 127 characters and is only really useful for Latin-based languages.

attribute   A named characteristic associated with an Extensible Markup Language (XML) element that supplies additional data about an element.

attribute-list declaration   A Document Type Declaration (DTD) listing of which attributes can be combined with a given element. A listing declaration includes the names of the attributes, their values and defaults (if applicable), and whether the attribute is required or optional.

attribute type   The value that specifies whether an attribute is a string, tokenized, or enumerated attribute.

attribute value   A list of all the possible values available for an attribute.

axis   The first section of each location path step in XPath, which specifies the correlation between a context node and the nodes chosen by the step.

bidirectional link   An XLink convention that allows a hyperlink to be navigated in more than one direction.

box properties   A group of Cascading Style Sheets (CSS) properties and values for an element that governs the element's margins, padding, height, width, and border aspects.

character entity   A series of characters used to correspond to other characters; for example, `&lt;` and `&quot;` show a string of characters (`lt` and `Egrave`) that stand for other characters (< and È).

character reference   Text used in a document to create declarations, markup, and text inside XML elements.

character set   A collection of values that map to a specific symbol set or alphabet.

child element   An element that is nested within another element; such an element also can be a parent of other, lower-level elements.

classification properties   A CSS property and value grouping that controls how white space and lists are presented.

comments   Notations in an XML document that are ignored by the XML processor.

content-based markup   Markup that describes information so that it can be processed by one or more applications or delivered aurally or in Braille.

content identifier   A token that uniquely distinguishes any piece of data or content.

CSS (Cascading Style Sheets)   A method of coding for defining how certain Hypertext Markup Language (HTML), dynamic HTML (DHTML), or XML elements, such as paragraphs and headings, should be displayed.

declaration   Specific markup that provides special instructions to the XML processor for how to process a document.

document element   The most important component of an XML document, the document element contains all the text and markup in the document. (Also called the *root element*.)

document type declaration   A piece of data that informs the processor of the DTD's location and contains declarations for a document. Also called the DOCTYPE declaration.

DOM (Document Object Model)   A programming interface that is platform- and language-neutral and that provides programs and scripts with access to the content, structure, and style of documents via a standard method.

DTD (Document Type Definition)   A specification for a document used to arrange structural elements and markup definitions so that they can be used to create documents.

EDI (Electronic Data Interchange)   An official standard used for the electronic exchange of basic business information.

element   A document component that consists of markup and the text contained within the markup.

element content model   A method for including a specification regarding child elements in element declarations.

element type   A named element, such as `<Book>` or `<Title>`.

element type declaration   A description of an element type and its content within the DTD.

extended link   A link stored in an external file that can have relationships with more than two resources.

font properties   CSS properties and values that specify font information for document elements.

HTML (Hypertext Markup Language)   A markup language used to create Web pages for display on the Internet or an intranet.

HTTP (Hypertext Transfer Protocol)   The Web protocol that provides communication between a Web server and a Web browser (uses HTML).

hypertext   A method for linking document locations. By clicking hypertext element, a user is sent to another location that can be within the same document or another Web document.

inheritance   The process of a child or sibling element being assigned (inheriting) the characteristics assigned to the parent element.

in-line styles   A style that is applicable to an XML document element.

internal DTD subset   The piece of a document's DTD included within a document.

intranet   An private, internal network that uses Internet protocols and standards.

ISO-Latin-1   The default character set used by XML and HTML. (Also known as *ISO 8859-1*.)

Java   Sun Microsystems' object-oriented programming language used for Web application development.

Java class files   The file or set of files containing instructions for a Java applet or application.

JavaScript   A scripting language used on Web pages.

metadata   Literally, data about data. Specifically, metadata contain defined elements for describing a document's structure, content, or rendering.

metalanguage   A language, such as XML and SGML, that communicates information about the language itself. Metalanguages are used to create other languages.

MIME (Multipurpose Internet Mail Extensions)   An e-mail standard that allows messages to include multiple types of data (such as binary, audio, video, and graphics) as attachments. MIME types also identify document types during transfers over the Web.

MSXML (Microsoft XML)   Microsoft's XML parser for Internet Explorer.

multidirectional link   A link that can be traversed in more than one direction.

namespace   A set of element types and attribute names.

nesting   The process of elements containing other elements in a hierarchical form.

node   A portion of an XML tree structure.

node-set function   An XPath function used in location paths to define the members of a node set.

notation   An XML declaration that connects a type of unparsed entity, such as a JPEG image, with a processing application, such as a graphics program.

notation declaration   Information that associates a notation name with data to identify an information interpreter described by the notation.

numeric entity   A set of numbers used to represent a character. Numeric entities are identified by an ampersand followed by a pound sign (#). (Also called *character references*.)

parameter entity   A DTD entity used to create an alias for a group of elements in the DTD.

parent element   An element that contains child elements.

parsed entity   Character data assigned as content for an entity name.

parser   An application that breaks an XML document into an element tree and checks its syntax.

PCDATA (parsed character data)   Plain-text element content.

PDF (Portable Document Format)   Adobe Systems' graphics file format that requires the Adobe Acrobat Reader, PageMaker, or Photoshop for display.

Perl   A common CGI programming language.

presentation-based markup   Markup, such as HTML, that describes text to be rendered by a browser.

pull technology   A method for a browser to retrieve information from a Web server.

push technology   A method for initiating content delivery from a server to a client.

RDF (Resource Description Framework)   An XML vocabulary for describing Internet resources, which provides a mechanism for organizing, describing, and navigating Web sites.

remote resource   A resource, such as a document, image, or sound file, at a location other than the document that contains the link.

result tree   The structure of elements and element content in a document.

root element   An XML element that is equivalent to the <html> element in HTML. Also called the document element.

schema   A pattern for representing the data's model that defines the elements (or objects), their attributes (or properties), and the relationships among the elements.

scripting language   A programming language for creating Web page scripts that controls various elements of the page, such as the user interface, styles, and markup.

selector   One part of a CSS style rule that defines the markup element to which the style rule is applied.

SGML (Standard Generalized Markup Language)   A text-based metalanguage for describing document content and structure.

simple link   A link in XML that uses the href attribute to point to a resource.

source tree   The structure of elements and element content in an XSLT document.

SQL (Structured Query Language)   IBM's language for relational database communications.

style rule   An XML document directive that specifies a pattern and an action to take when the specified pattern is found.

style sheet   A template-style document that provides information about the organization and content of another document or set of documents.

template   The directives in an XSLT style sheet that manage how an element and its content are converted.

text properties   CSS properties and values that detail text specifics for document elements.

traversal   Using a link in XLink to access a resource.

tree structure   A pyramid-shaped organizational scheme that is hierarchical.

Unicode character set   The ISO/IED 10646 standard 16-bit character encoding scheme. Unicode includes standard Roman and Greek alphabets, as well as mathematical symbols, special punctuation, and non-Roman alphabets, including Hebrew, Chinese, Arabic, Hangul, and other ideographic character sets.

UNIX   An interactive time-sharing operating system that is one of the most powerful multiuser operating systems available.

unparsed entity   A resource that isn't XML-encoded, such as audio and video files (which are binary entities).

URI (Uniform Resource Identifier)   A character string that identifies the type and location of an Internet resource.

valid XML document   A document that adheres to its DTD and is well formed.

validating parser   An application that checks an XML document for validity; it checks the document's DTD or schema and whether the document conforms to it.

VBScript (Visual Basic Scripting Edition) Microsoft's scripting language, similar to Visual Basic. VBScript is used only in Microsoft Web products.

W3C (World Wide Web Consortium) The association that is responsible for developing Web standards.

well-formed document An XML document that goes by the rules established in the XML specification that outline what makes a document well formed.

white space Certain blank areas of a document created by spaces or paragraphs that do not contain text or graphics.

XHTML (Extensible Hypertext Markup Language) The current recommendation from the W3C for merging HTML version 4 (for the vocabulary of elements) and XML (for syntax).

XLink (XML Linking Language) A language in XML documents that established instructions that describe the links among objects.

XML (Extensible Markup Language) A system for defining, validating, and sharing document formats.

XML application An XML implementation that is a DTD or set of DTDs designed to serve a specific purpose. (Also known as an *XML vocabulary*.)

XML declaration Information that informs the processor about which XML version to use for processing an XML document, which details the type of character encoding to be used for the document and whether the XML document is a standalone document.

XML entity Characters that allow a viewer to present a symbol yet not interpret it as markup.

XML namespace A prefix identifier that links an XML markup element to a specific DTD.

XML processor An application for reading and editing XML documents.

XML Schema A method of describing XML markup using XML notation.

XML specification A depiction that details how elements are declared and how XML must be constructed for XML processors (which interpret XML code) to process the XML information properly and send it to the Web browser for display.

XPath (XML Path Language) A language used by both XSL and XLink to address parts of XML documents.

XPointer (XML Pointer Language) A method of designating various resources by using terms that specify locations in documents or resources. XPointer is a companion to Xlink.

XSL (Extensible Stylesheet Language) A style sheet procedure customized for XML.

XSLT (XSL Transformations) An XSL component for providing a language for changing one XML document into another.

Internet and Networking Standards for XML

Internet standards for Extensible Markup Language (XML) and the languages that make up the XML family are easily incorporated into the framework of standards already established for the Hypertext Transfer Protocol (HTTP) and other components of the Internet and Web. The media types `text/xml`, `application/xml`, `text/xml-external-parsed-entity`, `application/xml-external-parsed-entity`, and `application/xml-dtd` are defined in the Internet Engineering Task Force's (IETF's) Request for Comments (RFC) 3023, which defines these five media types as XML Multipurpose Internet Mail Extensions (MIME) entities. MIME entities are transferred via HTTP over the Web.

B.1   Summary of MIME Types for XML

The lists and definitions in this section are extracted from RFC 3023 section 3.6; the full text of this document is online at `http://www.ietf.org/rfc/rfc3023.txt`.

The following list applies to `text/xml`, `text/xml-external-parsed-entity`, and XML-based media types under the top-level type "`text`" that define the `charset` parameter according to this specification:

- The `charset` parameter is strongly recommended.
- If the `charset` parameter is not specified, the default is "`us-ascii`". The default of "`iso-8859-1`" in HTTP is explicitly overridden.
- No error-handling provisions exist.

- An encoding declaration, if present, is irrelevant, but when saving a received resource as a file, the correct encoding declaration *should* be inserted.

The next list applies to `application/xml`, `application/xml-exter-nal-parsed-entity`, `application/xml-dtd`, and XML-based media types under top-level types other than `"text"` that define the `charset` parameter according to this specification:

- The `charset` parameter is strongly recommended, and if present, it takes precedence.
- If the `charset` parameter is omitted, conforming XML processors *must* follow the requirements of XML.

text/xml

The distinct MIME types are defined as follows in RFC 3023 section 3.1:

- MIME media type name: `text`
- MIME subtype name: `xml`
- Mandatory parameters: none
- Optional parameters: `charset`

Although listed as an optional parameter, use of the `charset` parameter is strongly recommended because this information can be used by XML processors to determine authoritatively the character encoding of the XML MIME entity. The `charset` parameter also can be used to provide protocol-specific operations, such as charset-based content negotiation in HTTP.

UTF-8 (RFC 2279) is the recommended value, representing the UTF-8 charset. UTF-8 is supported by all conforming processors of XML. If the XML MIME entity is transmitted via HTTP, which uses a MIME-like mechanism, this is exempt from the restrictions on the text top-level type. For more information, see Section 19.4.1 of RFC 2616; UTF-16 (RFC 2781) is also recommended. UTF-16 is supported by all conforming processors of XML. Because the handling of CR, LF, and NUL for text types in most MIME applications would cause undesired transformations of individual octets in UTF-16 multioctet characters, gateways from HTTP to these MIME applications *must* transform the XML MIME entity from `text/xml; charset="utf-16"` to `application/xml; char-set="utf-16"`. Conformant with RFC 2046, if a `text/xml` entity is received with the `charset` parameter omitted, MIME processors and XML processors *must* use the default `charset` value of `"us-ascii"` (ASCII).

In cases where the XML MIME entity is transmitted via HTTP, the default `charset` value is still `"us-ascii"`. (*Note:* There is an inconsistency between this specification and HTTP 1.1, which uses ISO-8859-1 as the default for a historical reason. Because XML is a new format, a new default should be chosen for better I18N.) US-ASCII was chosen because it is the intersection of UTF-8 and ISO-8859-1 and because it is already used by MIME.

There are several reasons that the `charset` parameter is authoritative:

- Some MIME processing engines do transcoding of MIME bodies of the top-level media type `text` without reference to any of the internal content. Thus it is possible that some agent might change `text/xml; charset ="iso-2022-jp"` to `text/xml; charset="utf-8"` without modifying the encoding declaration of an XML document.

- `text/xml` must be compatible with `text/plain` because MIME agents that do not understand `text/xml` will fall back to handling it as `text/plain`. If the `charset` parameter for `text/xml` were not authoritative, such fallback would cause data corruption.

- Recent Web servers have been improved so that users can specify the `charset` parameter.

- RFC 2130 specifies that the recommended specification scheme is the `charset` parameter. Because the `charset` parameter is authoritative, the charset is not always declared within an XML encoding declaration. Thus special care is needed when the recipient strips the MIME header and provides persistent storage of the received XML MIME entity (for example, in a file system). Unless the charset is UTF-8 or UTF-16, the recipient also should persistently store information about the charset, perhaps by embedding a correct XML encoding declaration within the XML MIME entity.

- This media type can be encoded as appropriate for the charset and the capabilities of the underlying MIME transport. For 7-bit transports, data in UTF-8 *must* be encoded in quoted-printable or base64. For 8-bit clean transport (for example, 8BITMIME RFC 1652, ESMTP, or NNTP RFC 0977), UTF-8 does not need to be encoded. Over HTTP, no content transfer encoding is necessary, and UTF-16 also may be used.

- XML has proven to be interoperable across WebDAV clients and servers and for import and export from multiple XML authoring tools. For maximum interoperability, validating processors are recommended. Although nonvalidating processors may be more efficient, they are not required to handle all features of XML.
  - The published specification is Extensible Markup Language (XML) 1.0 (second edition).
  - XML is device-, platform-, and vendor-neutral and is supported by a wide range of Web user agents, WebDAV (RFC 2518) clients and servers, and XML authoring tools.

- See Section 10 of RFC 3023 for security considerations.

- Additional information:
  - File extension(s): `.xml`
  - Macintosh file type code(s): `"TEXT"`

application/xml

Section 3.5 of RFC 3023:

- MIME media type name: `application`
- MIME subtype name: `xml`
- Mandatory parameters: none
- Optional parameters: `charset`

Although listed as an optional parameter, use of the `charset` parameter is strongly recommended because this information can be used by XML processors to determine authoritatively the charset of the XML MIME entity. The `charset` parameter also can be used to provide protocol-specific operations, such as charset-based content negotiation in HTTP. `"utf-8"` (RFC 2279) and `"utf-16"` (RFC 2781) are the recommended values, representing the UTF-8 and UTF-16 charsets, respectively. These charsets are preferred because they are supported by all conforming processors of XML.

If an `application/xml` entity is received in which the `charset` parameter is omitted, no information is being provided about the charset by the MIME content-type header. Conforming XML processors must follow the requirements of XML that directly address this contingency. However, MIME processors that are not XML processors should not assume a default charset if the `charset` parameter is omitted from an `application/xml` entity.

There are several reasons that the `charset` parameter is authoritative:

- Recent Web servers have been improved so that users can specify the `charset` parameter.
- RFC 2130 specifies that the recommended specification scheme is the `charset` parameter.

On the other hand, it has been argued that the `charset` parameter should be omitted and the mechanism described in Appendix F of the W3C's XML (which is nonnormative) should be relied on solely. This approach would allow users to avoid configuration of the `charset` parameter; an XML document stored in a file is likely to contain a correct encoding declaration or BOM (if necessary) because the operating system typically does not provide charset information for files. If users want to rely on the encoding declaration or BOM and to hide charset information from protocols, they may determine not to use the parameter.

Because the `charset` parameter is authoritative, the charset is not always declared within an XML encoding declaration. Thus special care is needed when the recipient strips the MIME header and provides persistent storage of the received XML MIME entity (for example, in a file system). Unless the charset is UTF-8 or UTF-16, the recipient also *should* persistently store information about the charset, perhaps by embedding a correct XML encoding declaration within the XML MIME entity.

Here are some encoding considerations:

- This media type can be encoded as appropriate for the charset and the capabilities of the underlying MIME transport.
- For 7-bit transports, data in either UTF-8 or UTF-16 *must* be encoded in quoted-printable or base64.

- For 8-bit clean transport, UTF-8 is not encoded, but the UTF-16 family must be encoded in base64.
- For binary clean transports [e.g., HTTP (RFC 2616)], no content transfer encoding is necessary.

Otherwise, security and interoperability considerations, the published specification, and applications that use this media type are the same as for `text/xml`.

text/xml-external-parsed-entity

Section 3.3 of RFC 2023:

- MIME media type name: `text`
- MIME subtype name: `xml-external-parsed-entity`
- Mandatory parameters: none
- Optional parameters: `charset`

The `charset` parameter of `text/xml-external-parsed-entity` is handled the same as that of `text/xml`, as described in `text/xml`. The encoding and security considerations are the same as for `text/xml`, as are the published specification and applications that use this media type. As for interoperability considerations, XML external parsed entities are as interoperable as XML documents, although they have a less tightly constrained structure and therefore need to be referenced by XML documents for proper handling by XML processors. Similarly, XML documents cannot be used reliably as external parsed entities because external parsed entities are prohibited from having standalone document declarations or DTDs. Identifying XML external parsed entities with their own content type should enhance interoperability of both XML documents and XML external parsed entities. In addition, supported file extensions are `.xml` and `.ent`, and the Macintosh file type code is `"TEXT"`.

application/xml-external-parsed-entity

Section 3.4 of RFC 2023:

- MIME media type name: `application`
- MIME subtype name: `xml-external-parsed-entity`
- Mandatory parameters: none
- Optional parameters: `charset`

The `charset` parameter of `application/xml-external-parsed-entity` is handled the same as that of `application/xml`, as described in `application/xml`. Interoperability considerations are the same as those for `text/xml-external-parsed-entity`, as described in `application/xml`. The published specification and applications that use this media type are the same as for `text/xml`.

application/xml-dtd

Section 3.5 of RFC 2023:

- MIME media type name: `application`
- MIME subtype name: `xml-dtd`
- Mandatory parameters: none
- Optional parameters: `charset`

The `charset` parameter of `application/xml-dtd` is handled the same as that of `application/xml`, as described in `application/xml`. Encoding considerations are the same as those for `application/xml`. Security considerations are the same as for `text/xml`. XML DTDs have proven to be interoperable by DTD authoring tools and XML browsers, among others. The published specification is the same as for `text/xml`. Applications that use this media type include DTD authoring tools that handle external DTD subsets as well as external parameter entities. XML browsers also may access external DTD subsets and external parameter entities. Finally, file extensions are `.dtd` or `.mod`, and the Macintosh file type code(s) is `"TEXT"`.

Online Resources

This appendix is a compilation of various online resources for XML.

CSS (Cascading Style Sheets)

Cascading Style Sheets: http://www.w3.org/Style/CSS/
Cascading Style Sheets, Level 2: http://www.w3.org/TR/REC-CSS2/
CSS3 module text:
  http://www.w3.org/TR/2001/WD-css3-text-20010517/

DOM

Document Object Model (DOM):
  http://www.oasis-open.org/cover/dom.html
DOM views: http://www.w3.org/TR/2000/REC-DOM-Level-2-
  Views-20001113/views.html
Content models and validation: http://www.w3.org/TR/2001/WD-DOM-
  Level-3-CMLS-20010209/content-models.html
DOM core: http://www.w3.org/TR/2000/REC-DOM-Level-2-Core-
  20001113/core.html
DOM activity statement: http://www.w3.org/DOM/Activity

General XML

*Links to the Recommendations and World Wide Web Consortium (W3C) docu-
  ments:* http://www.w3.org/
XML developer news from XMLhack: http://www.xmlhack.com
Café con Leche XML news and resources:
  http://www.ibiblio.org/xml/
A warehouse of XML information:
  http://xml.startkabel.nl

Schemas

SCHEMA.NET: http://www.schema.net
XML Schema Part 0 primer: http://www.w3.org/TR/xmlschema-0/

XML Schema Part 1 structures: http://www.w3.org/TR/xmlschema-1/
XML Schema Part 2 datatypes: http://www.w3.org/TR/xmlschema-2/
Metadata at W3C: http://www.w3.org/Metadata/

Tools and Tutorials

Free XML tools and software:
    http://www.garshol.priv.no/download/xmltools/
W3Schools online web tutorials: http://www.w3schools.com/
ZVON.org tutorials: http://www.zvon.org/index.php

XLink, XPointer, and XBase

XML Linking Language (XLink) version 1.0:
    http://www.w3.org/TR/xlink/
XML Linking Language (XLink) design principles:
    http://www.w3c.org/TR/NOTE-xlink-principles
XML Pointer Language (XPointer) version 1.0:
    http://www.w3.org/TR/xptr/
XML Base: http://www.w3c.org/TR/xmlbase/

XML Security

XML signature syntax and processing:
    http://www.w3.org/TR/xmldsig-core/#XML-Signature-RD
XML signature requirements:
    http://www.w3.org/TR/xmldsig-requirements
The XML Security Suite from IBM developerWorks XML zone:
    http://www-106.ibm.com/developerworks/library
    /xmlsecuritysuite/
XML and encryption:
    http://www.oasis-open.org/cover/xmlAndEncryption.html
XML encryption syntax and processing:
    http://www.w3.org/Encryption/2001/03/12-proposal

XPath

XQuery 1.0 and XPath 2.0 data model:
    http://www.w3.org/TR/2001/WD-query-datamodel-20010607

XSL and XSLT

The Extensible Stylesheet Language (XSL):
    http://www.w3.org/Style/XSL/
XSL Transformations (XSLT) version 1.1:
    http://www.w3.org/TR/xslt11/

Binary Math and Internet Protocol (IP) Address Calculation

Binary math (the base 2 system) forms the basis for all computer functions as we currently know it. It plays a vital role in Internet Protocol (IP) addressing scenarios. As you may already know, binary math is a system that performs numerical and arithmetic computation using two numbers (or states), the 0 and the 1. The entire system uses only these two digits, and any base 10 (the usual system) number can be expressed in binary by performing some reasonably simple conversions.

Position Reference	Power of 2	Decimal Equivalent
a	0	1
b	1	2
c	2	4
d	3	8
e	4	16
f	5	32
g	6	64
h	7	128

Each position from right to left represents a power of 2. The far-right digit is 2 to the first power (2^1), followed to the left by 2 to the second power (2^2), and so on. The preceding table provides an overview of the first eight positions using letters to represent the position.

Using this chart, you can convert between the systems (at least for the first eight places). Let's take, for example, 00010101. One method is to add up the decimal equivalents (per position) for each 1 that is found. In this case, starting at the right:

```
1 = 1 (a)
0 = 0 (b)
1 = 4 (c)
0 = 0 (d)
1 = 16 (e)
0 = 0 (f)
0 = 0 (g)
0 = 0 (h)
```

This yields the following: 1 + 4 + 16 = 21.

Let's look at another example, this time 10011101:

```
1 = 1 (a)
0 = 0 (b)
1 = 4 (c)
1 = 8 (d)
1 = 16 (e)
0 = 0 (f)
0 = 0 (g)
1 = 128 (h)
```

This yields the result of 1 + 4 + 8 + 16 + 128 = 157.

This system extends out to the left to infinity, but for IP addressing purposes, eight digits will do. This is so because a 1 in every position (11111111) is equal to 255 (decimal):

```
1 = 1 (a)
1 = 2 (b)
1 = 4 (c)
1 = 8 (d)
1 = 16 (e)
1 = 32 (f)
1 = 64 (g)
1 = 128 (h)
```

This equals 1 + 2 + 4 + 8 + 16 + 32 + 64 + 128 = 255.

The IP addressing scheme used in Internet Protocol version 4 (IPv4) uses primary addresses that extend to 255.255.255.255 or an 8-bit binary number for each value in the four number groups. As of this writing, there is limited support for but a lot of discussion around a six-group system (IPv6). For now, however, four will do.

Looking at some common addresses, the binary equivalents can be resolved by a similar process to the creation process just discussed. To convert from decimal (base 10) to binary (base 2), the decimal number is divided by decreasing powers of 2 until the value for 2^1 (1) is set.

Here is another table to help with this process (up through 2^7, or 255):

Decimal Equivalent	Power of 2	Position
128	7	h
64	6	g
32	5	f
16	4	e
8	3	d
4	2	c
2	1	b
1	0	a

If the decimal can be divided by the value in the left column, then a 1 is put in the position in the right column. If the quotient is more than 1, then use the next largest value in the left column. Keep dividing the remainder with ever-decreasing values from the left, and enter a 0 or a 1 in the position represented in the right column until 0 remains. Let's take the decimal numeral value 237 as an example.

```
237/128 = 1  (h) then 237 128 = 109
109/64 = 1   (g) then 109 64 = 45
45/32 = 1    (f) then 45 32 = 13
13/16 = 0    (e)
13/8 = 1     (d) then 13 8 = 5
5/4 = 1      (c) then 5 4 = 1
1/2 = 0      (b)
1/1 = 1      (a) then 1 1 = 0
```

Placing the 0s or 1s in position (from h at left) yields 11101101, which is the binary value for 237 decimal. Let's look at another example, this time for decimal 122.

```
122/128 = 0  (h)
122/64 = 1   (g) then 122 64 = 58
58/32 = 1    (f) then 58 32 = 26
26/16 = 1    (e) then 26 16 = 10
10/8 = 1     (d) then 10 8 = 2
2/4 = 0      (c)
2/2 = 1      (b) then 2 2 = 0
```

```
0/1 = 0    (a)
```

Placing the 0s or 1s in position (from h at left) yields 01111010, which is the binary value for 122 decimal.

It may be obvious by now that every digit added to the left side of the binary system accommodates almost a doubling of the decimal equivalent capacity. If (i) is added to the left of (h) in our model, the value is 2 to the eighth power (2^8), or 256 decimal. This gives a decimal capacity of 256 + 255, for a total of 511. Adding (j) as 2^9 (512) sets the capacity to 1023. This adding a position adds a bit to the binary value, so the original (ah) 8-bit value becomes a 9-bit value by adding (i) and a 10-bit value by adding (j). The processes for creating binary numbers and converting between decimal and binary remain the same, just another bit (or more) position and value are added to the table.

The Web (and the Internet at large) uses the Transmission Control Protocol/ Internet Protocol (TCP/IP) for information exchange. As mentioned earlier, this is currently based on four groups of three digits each, separated by a dot (.) character (commonly referred to as *dotted-quad notation*). These groups of three digits represent 0 to 255 as the decimal equivalent of an 8-bit binary number, not 0 to 999 in decimal, for a maximum of 255.255.255.255.

The following format is used to represent an IP address:

```
ppp.qqq.rrr.sss
```

which would represent, for instance:

```
216.182.123.118
```

The binary equivalent is

```
11011000.10110110.01111011.01110110
ppp = 11011000 (216)
qqq = 10110110 (182)
rrr = 01111011 (123)
sss = 01110110 (118)
```

Blocks of IP addresses are divided into network classes, designated as class A, class B, and class C. These classes determine the number of hosts per network, as well as the maximum number of networks. The ppp value sets the network class (A, B, or C), and subsequent hosts are set by the following three groups. Additionally, there are broadcast addresses for each class, which are shown in the following table:

Class	ppp	qqq	rrr	sss	Number of Possible Networks	Number of Possible Hosts	Standard Network Address	Standard Broadcast Address
A	*Net* 1−126	*Host* 1−254	*Host* 1−254	*Host* 1−254	126	16,387,064	ppp.0.0.0	ppp.255.255.255

B	*Net* 128–191	*Net* 1–254	*Host* 1–254	*Host* 1–254	16,256	64,516	ppp.qqq.0.0	ppp.qqq.255.255
C	*Net* 192–223	*Net* 1–254	*Net* 1–254	*Host* 1–254	2,064,512	254	ppp.qqq.rrr.0	ppp.qqq.rrr.255

However, there are blocks of addresses that are not used for the Internet but instead are used for internal networks:

Class	Start IP Address	End IP Address	Default *Subnet* Mask
A	10.0.0.0	10.255.255.255	255.0.0.0
B	172.16.0.0	172.31.25.255	255.255.0.0
C	192.168.1.0	192.168.255.255	255.255.255.0

By looking at these tables, a pattern to the addressing begins to emerge by the class and host designations. The most common Web domain class is class C, with over 2 million possible networks, each having 254 possible hosts, giving a total (for class C) of 528 million hosts. Unfortunately, this is not enough.

In a static IP scenario, each machine receives a unique static address, which uses up addresses in a hurry. For client-side use, a scheme such as the Dynamic Host Configuration Protocol (DHCP) or other dynamic IP assignment scenario is used to assign addresses on an as-needed basis, which helps remedy this addressing limitation.

For networks under a primary host (one of the 524 million), the addresses can be stretched by applying a subnet mask. Adding the mask to an IP address splits the address range that is assigned to host addresses and creates a new network and a subnet. A subnet mask (also called a *netmask*) can range from 0.0.0.0 to 255.255.255.255, with defaults listed in the preceding table.

The default subnet mask for a class C network is 255.255.255.0 (decimal) and 11111111.11111111.11111111.00000000 (binary). When applied to a class C address, this creates 2^8 or 256 new subnetworks. This indicates 256 hosts for the IP address 216.182.123.*. Using the preceding address, 216.182.123.118 or binary 11011000.10110110.01111011.01110110, we can perform a bitwise AND operation to each digit in the binary IP address to create the subnets. A bitwise AND works like so:

First Binary Number (IP Address)	Second Binary Number (Mask)	*Bitwise AND* Result
0	0	0
0	1	0
1	0	0
1	1	1

Therefore:

11011000.10110110.01111011.01110110 (IP) = 216.182.123.118

11111111.11111111.11111111.00000000 (mask) = 255.255.255.0

11011000.10110110.01111011.00000000 (result) = 216.182.123.0

This creates 254 new networks available to be assigned to address 216.182.123.0, reserving 216.182.123.255 as the broadcast address (which sends packets to all hosts on the network) and 216.182.123.0 for the network.

NOTE: If there aren't eight binary digits in any section of the IP address, 0s need to be padded to the left of the digits to make eight. You do not have to use 255.255.255.0 for the subnet mask; it is only specified as the default value. However, it is the most common value.

Using the conversion from binary to decimal (and back) and the bitwise AND operation allows most of the calculations needed for determining network scale and resources, as well as assigning IP addresses within a network. By following some simple rules (for example, the proper mask for each class network), you can be reasonably secure in knowing that there will not be addressing conflicts with other networks.

Keep in mind that IP or network addresses cannot be assigned at random. It is advisable to consult a good reference text on TCP/IP and networking before embarking on a project such as this. There are a few simple rules for subnetting:

- All hosts in the network must agree on the mask used.
- No two different subnets can use the same host address.
- The first (*.*.*.0) and last (*.*.*.255) numbers are reserved.
- The subnet cannot be all 1s in binary form.

For much more detailed information, see the relevant RFCs:

- *RFC 917:* "Internet Subnets"
- *RFC 950:* "Internet Standard Subnetting Procedure"
- *RFC 1517:* "Applicability Statement for the Implementation of Classless Inter-Domain Routing (CIDR)"
- *RFC 1518:* "An Architecture for IP Address Allocation with CIDR"

- *RFC 1519:* "Classless Inter-Domain Routing (CIDR): An Address Assignment and Aggregation Strategy"
- *RFC 1520:* "Exchanging Routing Information Across Provider Boundaries in the CIDR Environment"
- *RFC 1878:* "Variable Length Subnet Table For IPv4"

Bibliography

GENERAL XML

Beginning XML, by David Hunter. Wrox Press, Birmingham, U.K., 2000, ISBN 1-861-0034-1-2.

Essential XML Beyond Markup, by Don Box, Aaron Skonnard, and John Lam. Addison-Wesley, Upper Saddle River, NJ, 2000, ISBN 0-201-70914-7.

XML A Primer, 2d ed, by Simon St. Laurent. M & T Books, Foster City, CA, 1999, ISBN 0-764-53310-X.

XML Black Book, 2d ed., by Natanya Pitts. Coriolis Group, Scottsdale, AZ, 2001, ISBN 1-576-10783-3.

XML By Example, by Benoit Marchal. Que Books, Indianapolis, IN, 2000, ISBN 0-789-72242-9.

The XML Companion, by Neil Bradley. Addison-Wesley, Upper Saddle River, NJ, 2000, ISBN 0-201-67486-6.

XML Elements of Style, by Simon St. Laurent. McGraw-Hill, New York, 2000, ISBN 0-07-212220-X.

XML in a Nutshell, by Elliote Rusty Harold and W. Scott Means. O'Reilly & Associates, Sebastopol, CA, 2001, ISBN 0-596-00058-8.

OTHER XML LANGUAGES

Professional XML Schemas, by Cagle et al. Wrox Press, Birmingham, U.K., 2001, ISBN 1-86100-547-4.

The XSL Companion, by Neil Bradley. Addison-Wesley, Upper Saddle River, NJ, 2000, ISBN 0-201-67487-4.

XSLT Programmer's Reference, by Michael Kay. Wrox Press, Birmingham, U.K., 2000, ISBN 1-86100-312-9.

XSLT Working with XML and HTML, by Khun Yee Fung. Addison-Wesley, Upper Saddle River, NJ, 2000, ISBN 0-201-71103-6.

INDEX